STITCHING UP
−PARIS−

*The Insider's Guide to Parisian Knitting,
Sewing, Notions and Needlecraft Stores*

Keep in Touch with *Stitching up Paris*

Follow our blog for the latest stories and images of the Paris stitching scene at
www.stitchingupparisblog.wordpress.com

To request your personal tailor-made Paris stitching tour with Barbara visit
www.stitchingupparis.com

Follow us on social media **@stitchingupparis** on:

CONTENTS

INTRODUCTION

Audrey Hepburn was right: 'Paris is always a good idea'. Magnificent holiday illuminations compensate for grey winter days when icy rain falls on weathered cobblestones. Spring brings a cascade of colours. Food artisans from chocolatiers to butchers exalt produce from regions near and far. The splendour explains why the French translate window shopping as *faire du lèche-vitrines*: window licking.

Stitching up Paris: The Insider's Guide to Parisian Knitting, Sewing, Notions and Needlecraft Stores offers crafters sixty-five more tempting reasons why Paris is always a good idea. Delightful boutiques, hidden warehouses, lively flea markets; the secret places where Parisians find glorious craft materials and finishing touches to create their signature handmade style.

Paris style is seen in the old stitched together with the new, traditional, elegant or edgy, kaleidoscopic or neutral. It comes from craftsmanship. A valued aspect of French heritage, artisan crafts are cherished and renewed with vigour. Modern fashion schools welcome eager students into tailoring, couture and design courses, skilled *passementerie* and embroidery artisans nurture apprentices on the job, antique fabrics and lace are treasures hunted down to reuse, passionate craftsmen and women revitalise old neighbourhood businesses for new generations of enthusiastic customers who esteem the handmade ethic.

About the Authors

Originating from New Zealand, and both having grown up in families where knitting and sewing skills were inherited along with a love for natural fibre textiles and yarns, Barbara and Keiry's kiwi do-it-yourself values have found a perfect home in Paris, a city that has cultivated artisan needlecrafts for centuries and values the notion of handmade in a fast fashion world.

A Parisian for more than 30 years, Barbara has made Paris craft shops and the people behind them into a livelihood. Through *Stitching up Paris* (www.stitchingupparis.com) she provides individually tailored tours of Paris's best craft addresses. Not only familiar with well-known boutiques and fabric stores, she knows out-of-the-way suppliers through her contacts with professional costumiers, has inside knowledge of wholesale fabric warehouses, and is a discerning scout of antique and vintage materials. Barbara's favourite craft is sewing; in particular she enjoys re-purposing old fabrics and notions discovered in flea markets.

Keiry arrived in Paris in 2012 and almost immediately bumped into Barbara on Ravelry's online knitting network. With more leisure time than ever before, Keiry explored the Parisian knitting scene and decided to indulge her creative aspirations by blogging about her Parisian life – including the perils of trying to speak French while knitting.

Two New Zealanders, stitchers, *flâneurs*, ardent handmade fans, it was inevitable that they became friends. This book is the result of a shared passion for artisan needlecrafts and a wish to put the make-it-yourself treasures of Paris within everyone's grasp.

This book is made for you to revel in your crafting passion while you explore Paris on a trip or from your armchair. Indulge your senses and dive into your favourite craft to discover beautiful fabrics or glorious knitting yarns, elegant needlework or romantic vintage laces and linens, beads and ribbons or old-fashioned notions. With a bundle of un-missable Paris addresses gathered together in one chapter for each craft, *Stitching up Paris* is designed for you to luxuriate in the creative ambience of Paris, craft by craft without needing to rummage through the pages or the city.

Monique Lyonnet from La Croix et La Manière told us that she felt privileged to have made her career – her *métier* – in the pastimes of others. Likewise it is our pleasure and privilege to celebrate the Parisian world of needlecrafts and make-it-yourself with you. Bon voyage and happy stitching.

Stitching up Paris is organised by craft with each chapter including personal stories of enterprising and talented craftsmen and women, notes about their neighbourhood and insights into the indelible marks of French history on textile crafts and Parisian life. As, like ourselves, many crafters have more than one textile craft interest we have included a list of stores organised by district to help you plan your very own stitching tour. The journey is yours to customise. The addresses are indexed by district *(arrondissement)* and alphabetically and a glossary of terms can be found at the back of the book.

Shopping hours in Paris are not standard, particularly for small businesses such as those featured in this book. Many are closed one or two days per week, often Sundays, some close for lunch breaks and many have reduced hours or close for a month over summer. It is a good idea to check the shop's website and/or social media, for opening days and hours before heading out. We have included the current opening hours as advised to us by the owner at the time of publication.

For stores operating a website, we have included symbols to indicate if online sales and/or an English language version exist with 🗨 and 🖳 Many storeowners told us that they plan to sell online in the near future so it's worth rechecking in the future.

Please note that while we have taken great care to provide accurate information, Paris changes: shops close, merchandise is not constant, online addresses are updated or sometimes deleted. The authors and publishers of *Stitching up Paris* cannot be held responsible for facts that become outdated, nor for any inadvertent errors or omissions in this guide.

In the spirit of the make-it-yourself ethic we took the photographs in this book ourselves; they show Paris, its markets and streets, craft and textile supplies as they are. There are many other beautiful shops and interesting warehouses in Paris, we could not include every last one. We've handpicked a selection of destinations we think will be a good fit for a wide range of travellers interested in textile and needlecrafts, from armchair travellers to expats, residents and tourists making the most of precious time in this beautiful city.

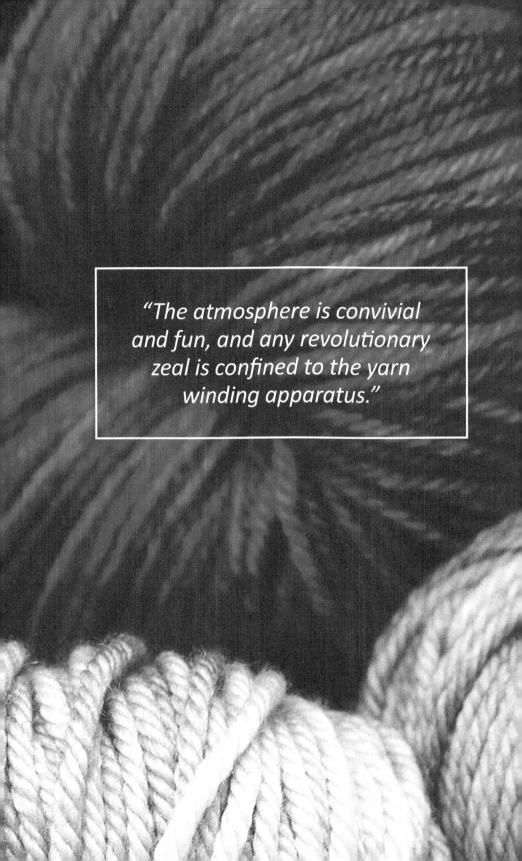

"The atmosphere is convivial and fun, and any revolutionary zeal is confined to the yarn winding apparatus."

KNITTING
AND YARN

Parisian knitters – *les tricoteuses* – have been famously depicted as callous, bloodthirsty old women, who supposedly knitted and cheered as they watched aristocratic heads topple at the guillotine in revolutionary Paris.

Parisian knitters have overcome such unflattering images. The knitters in our acquaintance are more accurately described as charming, chic and very talented. They are still very social; there are several knitting groups in the Paris area that meet regularly. The atmosphere is convivial and fun, and any revolutionary zeal is confined to the yarn winding apparatus.

LES TRICOTEURS VOLANTS

Enrico is a talented yarn man; he spins, he knits, he crochets. He is also the proud owner of the neighbourhood yarn shop Les Tricoteurs Volants on rue de la Fidélité; a bright spot in a bustling neighbourhood not far from Gare de L'Est.

First opened in 1932, it is the oldest yarn and haberdashery store in Paris. Enrico lives locally and noticed it was for sale at a time when he contemplated a career change. He says it was more of an "a-ha" moment than the realisation of a dream to own a yarn store. With moral support of friends and family he made the change from being a specialist in French literature at a bookstore to owner and creative specialist in a yarn store. He happens to be the Flying Knitter behind the name of the shop – a nickname he earned during the filming of a yarn-bombing project.

Enrico looks for natural fibre yarns produced locally for his shop. The range includes a number of attractive age-old French brands: Filature du Valgaudemar, Cheval Blanc, Bergère and Plassard, as well as interesting new brands from elsewhere in Europe and the UK; Treskilion from Wales and John Arbon textiles from Devon. There is a small quantity of yarn that is hand-spun in Paris. The shop is well provisioned with all the necessary accessories: Bergère, Knit Pro, Hiya Hiya and Addi knitting needles and crochet hooks, plus ribbons, buttons, embroidery threads and a selection of pattern books.

As the fifth owner, Enrico wants to serve his locality as well as be a sought-after destination for global knitters. The constant stream of shoppers from grannies and kids, men and women, to knitters on a mission and casual passers-by suggests he is doing just that.

22 Rue de la Fidélité, Paris 75010
Ph: 01 47 70 52 57
www.lestricoteursvolants.com
Open: 10.30am to 7.30pm
Tuesday to Saturday
Metro: Gare de L'Est

NEIGHBOURHOOD NOTES

Le Passage du Grand Cerf

From the early 19th century many covered passages were built to offer Parisians a more pleasant shopping experience away from noisy dirty streets and inclement weather, but by the end of the century the department stores took over as the fashionable places to shop and the passages fell into disrepair. Of several covered passages that remain in Paris, the Passage du Grand Cerf is often described as one of the most beautiful. It was renovated in the 1990s to accommodate attractive boutiques under a 12-metre high glass ceiling along its length. It's thought that the Passage du Grand Cerf originally housed artisan workshops rather than being primarily a shopping destination as the ceiling height permitted three levels in the passage: a top residential level, the middle level for workshops and the ground level for workshops and some retail.

Construction of the passage began in 1825 on the site that had been the Hôtellerie du Grand Cerf, which served as a relay station for the mail service. During the turbulent late 1820s rue St Denis was commonly the site of riots; barricades would be erected in the street and the passageways used as escape routes and refuges for the rebels. On one occasion a Parisian military squad quelled the street riot with a bayonet charge leaving several of the rebels dead in and around the passage du Grand Cerf.

Episode Vintage

At number 12 Rue Tiquetonne, 75002 this well-known second-hand store has a fast moving collection of vintage knits that on any one day can include Norwegian frogged jackets, Peruvian intarsia and 1950s lace cardigans.

LIL WEASEL

Located in the Passage du Grand Cerf – one of the most beautiful covered arcades in Paris – yarn and fabric boutique Lil Weasel is a sight to behold. Once you tear your eyes away from the architectural delight of the passage itself you notice bolts of pretty fabrics standing in the passageway, then through the big window the shelves full of yarn arranged in colourful drifts entice you in.

Lil Weasel's owner, Carine, opened her doors in 2010 after the space in the Passage had been empty for some time. The revival of the Passage and its surrounding area with chic little boutiques was serendipitously in tune with the revival of hand-knitting and needlecrafts that prompted Carine's decision to open her boutique in this space.

Lil Weasel offers a wide selection of yarn including the French brand Fonty, Rowan and Debbie Bliss from the UK, specialty yarns from the US and Canada, and European cottons for summer knitting. Apart from sock yarn, you won't find yarns with synthetic fibre content. In an exciting development Carine released her own Lil Weasel brand of quality 100% French merino wool in colours that match the range of France Duval Stalla fabric in her shop and more recently the Betsy yarn collection inspired by her favourite Liberty fabrics.

The range of yarns and fabrics appeals to doting mothers and grandmothers knitting and sewing for babes and children, as well as the new generation of Ravelry knitters creating modern accessories: shawls, scarves, mittens, socks and hats.

Lil Weasel's cheerful merchandise extends to practical-yet-fun knitting tools and sewing notions that make ideal lightweight gifts and souvenirs, easy to tuck into a suitcase for the trip home.

In case you are wondering, there is a story behind the name. Before having her first baby, the choice of a name agreeable to *maman* and *papa* was elusive, so they nicknamed their baby *la petite belette*. Yes, that's a little weasel, sounds so cute in French.

1 Passage du Grand Cerf, Paris 75002
Ph: 01 73 71 70 48
www.lilweasel.fr
Open: Tuesday to Saturday 10.30am to 7pm
Metro: Etienne Marcel

CAT'LAINE

Catherine, or Cat to her friends and family, knew when she was fifteen that she wanted to work among balls of wool, and that's exactly what she has done. However, she's done things a little differently and all in the name of customer enjoyment.

Fifteen years ago after having made a career in the yarn industry she opened her own boutique selling popular knitting and crochet yarns at discounted prices. As Catherine is a self-confessed yarn devotee and collector, the driving force behind her business venture is to make good-quality yarn available at a reasonable price.

Catherine negotiates with yarn manufacturers, spinning mills and wholesalers, buying end-of-line, un-labelled and sample yarns. She selects from the range of yarns on offer knowing her regulars prize quality, and as a result her shop brims with great bargains. Bright coloured balls explode from the boxes of gorgeous yarns stacked on shelves and on the floor; you can find fantasy fibres in all sorts of combinations, sequins and sparkles, merinos and mohairs, silk, alpaca, cashmere and pure wool, textured yarns and fine smooth cottons.

To inspire customers, Catherine designs garments and knits up a sample for display in her shop. Clients are able to buy the yarn and receive the pattern as part of the purchase. Aside from yarn, and cats, Catherine's passions are history and art; she takes inspiration for her designs from the works of her favourite artists: Matisse for colour and dynamism, the impressionists for more colour. Of course, in Paris she is never short of a wonderful museum or art gallery to stimulate her creative ideas.

19 Rue Saint-Marc, Paris 75002
Ph: 01 42 96 00 69
Open: Monday noon to 2pm, 2.30pm to 6pm. Tuesday to Friday 10am to 2pm, 2.30pm to 6pm, Saturday noon to 5pm.
Metro: Richelieu-Drouot

NEIGHBOURHOOD NOTES

Passage des Panoramas, Passage Jouffroy and Passage Verdeau

Walk from Cat' Laine to Le Comptoir to imitate the stylish 19th century citizens – *les flâneurs* – who had time to stroll through the fashionable covered passageways enjoying the opportunity to admire newly available luxury goods.

From the entrances to Passage des Panoramas on Rue Saint-Marc near Cat'Laine in the 2nd arrondissement it is possible to thread your way through three of the covered passages to exit in the 9th on Rue de la Faubourg-Montmartre not far from Le Comptoir on Rue Cadet.

The first of the three to be built, Passage des Panoramas with its long narrow corridors, is now filled with small cafés and eateries, some of which have attained a serious following from the gourmet crowd. Among a few remaining stamp collector shops and an assortment of retailers, Annie Guillemard's boutique at number 7 offers supplies and courses for framing and *cartonnage*.

Exit Passage des Panoramas and cross Boulevard Montmartre to enter Passage Jouffroy, which runs through to Rue de la Grange Batelière opposite the entrance to Passage Verdeau. Built together as part of the same development project in 1847, Jouffroy and Verdeau house a wonderful mix of retailers, the Paris wax museum Musée Grévin, cafes, restaurants and tea salons. The antique cane shop at number 34 radiates theatrical glamour and everyone flocks to the old-world toy shop opposite. Further along you can find antique postcards, prints and books, chocolate shops, jewellery and fashion boutiques. Embroiderers won't want to miss Le Bonheur des Dames at number 8 Passage Verdeau.

LE COMPTOIR

Just as it might have done in 1865, the bell dings when the door opens into Le Comptoir at 26 Rue Cadet. Barbara Legarsmeur's shop housed a tailoring business back in 1865 when the building was constructed.

The original handsome wooden counter – *le comptoir* – is still there and in exceptionally good condition. So too are the wooden shelves tidily stacked with balls of yarns, and rows of shallow drawers with old-fashioned brass handles that contain a myriad of essential supplies for needlecrafts.

With Rue Cadet not far from the Grand Boulevards and two of the popular covered passageways, Passage Verdeau and Passage Jouffroy, it's easy to imagine elegant Parisians being attended to in the original tailor's shop; with scissors snipping fabric on the long counter top, orders confirmed and delivery dates promised. Later, from 1936 until 2004 when Barbara took over the shop in partnership with her mother, it was a wholesaler's for tailoring supplies.

The sense of solidity, of long lasting quality and reliability is completely in keeping with the yarns, fabrics and needlecraft notions available at Le Comptoir. Among the yarn brands are Rowan, Debbie Bliss, Noro, Fonty, Adriafil, Plassard Alpaca, Handmaiden and Holst Garn. Clientele can caress the sample squares already knitted up in these yarns to test the softness, density and visualise their own future projects. There are beautiful buttons, trims, and embroidery materials, ribbons, sewing patterns and bags to hold handmade projects.

Barbara is full of admiration for the fine crochet work of Sophie Digard and sells her pieces through the shop. Tourists visit especially for the shawls, or a scarf, and it's not uncommon for hotel concierges to call on behalf of their guests searching for Sophie Digard pieces or yarn and needlecraft supplies.

Barbara adores the lively Rue Cadet neighbourhood and life in her boutique; it's a world away from where her law studies led her initially and fulfils a very different long time ambition. Le Comptoir is patronised by local office workers and residents as well as tourists from around the globe. As Barbara says, she serves very pleasant people, unhurried and courteous, who enjoy the pleasure of shopping for their creative pastimes.

26 rue Cadet, Paris 75009
Ph 01 42 46 20 72
www.lapetiteboutiqueducomptoir.com
Open: Tuesday to Saturday 11am to 2pm, 2.30pm to 7pm.
Metro: Cadet

NEIGHBOURHOOD NOTES

The Butte aux Cailles is well known
for its cool street art. Here and there
black and white sketches decorate
buildings with *une femme fatale* and a
few witty words giving an air of voguish
graffiti chic. There's a distinct village
atmosphere in the Butte, a pleasant
escape from the imposing grandeur of
the monument-filled city centre. Quirky
street cafes attract plenty of customers;
locals and students from around the
world enjoy the edgy ambience elbow to
elbow at popular spots like Chez Gladine
on Rue des Cinq Diamants.

Galerie des Gobelins and Manufactures des Gobelins

In the mid-17th century the French
government purchased the tapestry
workshops operating on the site where
almost a century earlier the Gobelins
family had established their wool-
dyeing workshop near the Bièvre River.
Considered an important manufacturing
skill for the French nation, tapestry making
by skilled craftsmen was developed by the
state and only interrupted during times
of economic hardship and revolution.
Today the workshops still produce a small
number of contemporary tapestries. The
Gobelins workshops operate under the
direction of the National Mobilier de
France, the government department within
the Ministry of Culture responsible for the
furnishing and decoration of state palaces
and institutions.

The gallery is open daily, reservations
are essential for the guided visit to the
manufacturing workshops offered on
Tuesdays, Wednesdays and Thursdays.
Check 'Practical Information'
details carefully at:
www.mobiliernational.culture.gouv.fr
Les Gobelins, 42 Avenue des Gobelins,
Paris 75013.
Metro: Les Gobelins or Place d'Italie

L'OISIVETHÉ

The name L'OisiveThé is a play on the French word meaning leisureliness; perfect for this charming little tea salon and yarn boutique. Inside, the atmosphere is a picture of leisurely activity. It's free of disruptive radio or jangling music.

Instead your senses are gently stimulated by the rainbow of precious skeins of Koigu yarn hanging on the wall and shelves brimming with sought after brands Madeline Tosh, Quince & Co, Sweet Georgia, Baa Ram Ewe, John Arbon and Blue Moon Fibre Arts. L'OisiveThé concentrates on high-quality hand-dyed and specialty yarn suppliers from the US, Canada and the UK, regularly introducing new yarns to the stock.

Nestled in the Butte aux Cailles village of the 13th arrondissement away from the hustle of tourist hot spots, L'OisiveThé is owned by American Aimee Osbourn-Gille. It really was a whirlwind of romance that lifted Aimee up and away from her home in Kansas and landed her in Paris. In the early years of her new life in Paris, she dreamed of owning a little non-smoking café where fellow knitters could knit, sip tea and enjoy precious leisure time. In 2007 she turned the dream into reality. Aimee spied a small 'For Sale' sign in a café window and knew instantly it was the right place for her. In quick time the purchase was settled, the tea salon refreshed and stocked with beautiful yarns and a four-strong group of faithful knitters met for the first *tricot-soirée*.

Aimee tests all the yarns she sells; knitting a hat or mittens for her children as a sample. L'OisiveThé offers everything knitters and crocheters need: project bags, needles and hooks, inspirational patterns from leading independent designers and friendly advice to get you started. Develop your own chic French style with ready to cast-on kits for lacy shawls, cowls and scarves and stay within your travel budget.

To accompany the clack-clack of your needles, indulge in one of the special aromatic teas with exotic sounding names served in pretty patterned teapots. L'OisiveThé offers lunch and brunch menus, as well as morning and afternoon tea with delicious cakes, scones and cookies, all made in-house.

10 Rue Butte aux Cailles / 1 rue Marie Jego, Paris 75013
Ph: 01 53 80 31 33
www.loisivethe.com
Open: Tuesday noon to 3pm, Wednesday to Friday noon to 6pm, Saturday and Sunday 11am to 6pm. Closed Monday.
Metro: Corvisart or Place d'Italie

ST DENIS MUSEUM OF ART &HISTORY

One of the earliest known pieces of European knitting, a 14th century knitted cap, can be seen in the museum section devoted to local archaeological finds at this former Carmelite convent. The precious cap is knitted in the round, in stocking stitch, using an extraordinary fibre originating from a Mediterranean shellfish, *Pinna nobilis*, known as sea-silk or byssus. This yarn was used for luxury items such as gloves and caps.

22 bis Avenue Gabriel Péri, St Denis 93200

Open: Monday, Wednesday and Friday 10am to 5.30pm, Thursday 10am to 8pm, Saturday and Sunday 2pm to 6.30pm
Metro: Saint-Denis-Porte de Paris

LA BIEN AIMÉE

This new sister shop of L'OisiveThé is located in the same neighbourhood, but is no carbon copy of the tea shop. A former photography studio, it ticked all the boxes for Aimee Osbourn-Gille's new venture into hand dyeing her own range of yarn. After converting the photo lab to a yarn lab, creating a pretty shop interior and painting the exterior in yellow that is bright enough to make every day sunny, Aimee opened the doors in summer 2015.

The new store has its own look and a dedicated space for group classes. The focus here is definitely on yarn, knitting and crochet with everything to create and finish exceptional projects: one-on-one lessons to get started, tutorials for problem solving, buttons that are just a bit different, nifty haberdashery and notions. Pretty project bags hand made in France and organic cotton tea towels printed with motifs for yarn lovers make delightful gifts for knitting friends, as do the winsome wooden sheep.

Yarns in stock here include De Rerum Natura from France, Jamieson's of Shetland, Woolfolk, Freia, Toft, Julie Asselin, The Fibre Company and the unique collection of La Bien Aimée yarns, hand-dyed in Paris. The two stores, La Bien Aimée and L'OisiveThé, function in perfect harmony. Daytime classes are held at La Bien Aimée, including creative workshops for kids, while evening classes and social knitting events take place at L'OisiveThé.

27 Rue Paulin Méry, Paris 75013
Ph: 01 46 27 60 86
www.labienaimee.com
(online store is through www.loisivethe.com)
Open: Tuesday, Thursday, Friday, Saturday noon to 6pm, Wednesday noon to 6.30pm. Closed Sunday and Monday.
Metro: Place d'Italie

LES PETITS POINTS PARISIENS

Knitting and numbers are a happy combination for Anne. As a former economist-accountant and a knitter-dressmaker since childhood she simply added together all her skills to launch her own business, Les Petits Points Parisiens, in 2012.

Anne found an ideal spot to open her knitting yarn and fabric boutique on Rue Veron, just one street over and parallel with Rue Abbesses in the heart of Montmartre village; a lively and fascinating part of Paris. The space even came with a pedigree for creative spirits as the former office for French film director / writer Jean Pierre Jeunet during the filming of *Amélie / Le Fabuleux Destin d'Amélie Poulain*.

The boutique has a wonderful sense of serenity; from the midnight blue-grey street façade to the interior furniture, all thoughtfully sourced from flea markets, second-hand and *brocante* stores. A pewter-coloured bottle-drying rack serves a new purpose holding cones of fine yarn, spacious open shelves hold yarn from suppliers Uncommon Thread, Madeleine Tosh, NBK, Malabrigo, Graine de Laines, Laine des Alpes and many more. Without even trying, all the soft greys, greens and neutral shades complement the look wonderfully.

Anne collaborates with young independent French designers to match new designs with Petits Points' yarn range. The design samples that decorate the shop are fall-in-love gorgeous.

In addition to knitting and crochet yarns there's a good range of quality fabrics: les Trouvailles d'Amandine, France Duval Stalla, Atelier Brunette, Liberty and organic French linen fabrics from Normandy. More offerings are in the pipeline including online yarn sales and new yarn suppliers.

Anne offers knitting and sewing classes and hosts knit night for up to sixteen people on Thursday evenings, with all the details for joining on Petits Points' Ravelry group page. *Amélie* would be right at home here, we think.

24 Rue Véron, Paris 75018
Ph: 01 72 34 77 37
www.lespetitspointsparisiens.com
Open: Monday 10.30am to 4pm, Tuesday 11am to 8.30pm, Thursday 11am to 10pm, Friday and Saturday 11am to 7pm. The boutique is open the first and last Sundays of each month 11am to 7pm.
Metro: Abbesses

SOCIAL KNITTING IN PARIS

There is nothing new about the social nature of knitting; groups of knitters have enjoyed getting together to craft in company since the first stitches were cast onto sticks. At the Musée Carnavalet, 16 Rue des Francs Bourgeois in the Marais district, the famous *Tricoteuses Jacobins* – the women knitters of the Revolution – feature in one of Jean-Baptiste Lesueur's paintings. This work is one of a series of small gouache paintings that tell the story of revolutionary Paris in cut out pictures. The women are drawn knitting red hats – the symbolic *bonnet rouge*.

Join up with a knitting group in Paris at L'OisiveThé or Les Petits Points Parisiens.

L'OisiveThé: weekly knit night, Wednesdays 6.30 pm to 10pm, 22 places available.

Tricot soirée on Wednesday evenings with food and refreshments from the café menu is now so popular there is sometimes a waiting list to attend. The regular attendees are a mix of French and English speakers. Holidaying visitors are welcome to join in for a convivial evening of knitting, crochet and conversation. To register, sign up on the L'OisiveThé Ravelry group page when the event is posted on the Sunday evening prior. Instructions for securing your place are on the group page in English and French.

Les Petits Points Parisiens: weekly knit night, Thursdays 6pm to 10pm, 16 places available

The friends of Petits Points get together on Thursday evening to share platters of finger food, cold meats, cheeses, refreshments and delicious cakes while working on current projects.

To register, follow the links on the Petits Points' Ravelry group page to sign up when the event is posted.

Bon tricot and bon appétit.

COUSINE

Here's another dainty little boutique that has recently emerged from the makeover of a long-standing neighbourhood haberdashery and wool shop. From yarns in delicate marshmallow pastels to rich dark-chocolate-coloured balls with a seam of golden toffee-coloured thread, everything at Cousine Mercerie looks delectable.

Cousine stocks yarns from Rico, Debbie Bliss, Fonty, Bouton d'Or, Annie Blatt, DMC and Adriafil: a superb selection of fantasy yarns, gigantic mohair, cottons and yarn with a bit of bling. Raphaelle, the delightful owner, offers weaving and knitting classes for beginners on a regular basis. She has found an artisan supplier to make wooden weaving looms for her shop. These are available in two sizes – small and even smaller – and are suitable for weaving cushion covers, scarves and

jewellery. Cousine also sells fun accessories like pompom makers, king-size Tricotins (the French knitting gizmos for children), buttons, ribbons and trims. There is plenty of fun to be had with yarn here.

30 Rue Saint-Ambroise, Paris 75011
Ph: 01 47 00 02 03
www.merceriecousine.com
Open: Tuesday to Saturday 10.30am to 7.30pm
Metro: Saint-Ambroise or Rue Saint-Maur

WEBER MÉTAUX

A vast engineering and industrial supply store, this is a veritable man cave. It might not be a destination you would expect to see in a book about the most attractive sewing, knitting and embroidery stores in Paris, but here it is and for good reason.

Since 1889, Weber Métaux has been a feature of the Marais district. It now finds itself incongruously among design stores and chic clothing boutiques in this trendy part of Paris. It's the place to go for fine metal threads already discovered by avant-garde fabric artists, couture and jewellery designers for creating extraordinary artworks and design pieces.

Various metal compositions and several gauges of wire are available; some so fine it will pass through the eye of a sewing needle, others for knitting, crochet and weaving. The metal thread is sold on bobbins or larger coils and priced by weight. Down in the basement the rows of gleaming enamel coated copper wires make an impressive display. No-fuss labels specify the wire gauge and metal composition: natural copper, gilded copper, tin plated and silver plated copper, titanium, softened steel are just a few of the options. There's even invisible wire for magicians and theatrical pyrotechnics, beads, charms and mesh tubing for jewellery work. Upstairs there's a selection of metal fabric – chainmail – for garments, bags, and belts. These materials are sold by the metre, by 10cm squares or in a large piece called a panel. Have fun exploring.

9 Rue Poitou, Paris 75003
www.weber-metaux.com
Open: Monday to Friday 8.30am to 5.30pm
Metro: Saint-Sébastien-Froissart or Filles du Calvaire

ADDRESSES TO STASH

Plassard, Phildar and Bergère de France yarns and patterns are classic French yarn brands.

Phildar boutiques

Passage de Provence, 96 rue de Provence, Paris 75009

68 Rue Monge, Paris 75005

BHV department store, 54 rue de Rivoli, Paris 75004

Bergère de France www.bergeredefrance.com

Also available at 88 Rue Lamarck, Paris 75018

Bergère de France and Phildar yarns are available at:

Tricot St Pierre, 2 rue Charles Nodier, 75018

Bergère de France, Plassard and Fonty yarns are available at:

Une Maille à l'Endroit boutiques www.unemaillealendroit.com

57 Rue Monge, Paris 75005

12 Place Adolphe Chérioux, Paris 75015

87 Rue de Lévis, Paris 75017

"Paris needs no introduction as the capital of haute couture. It has long been the place to go for the art of fashionable dressing."

FABRICS
AND SEWING

Paris needs no introduction as the capital of haute couture.
It has long been the place to go for the art of fashionable
dressing. Even before Mr. Charles Worth (an Englishman in fact)
set up the first luxury dressmaking business in the middle of the
19th century, earning the term 'fashion designer', people have
been drawn to Paris for its inherent style. Jean Paul Gaultier
moved to Paris as a teenager, bought fabrics he could afford at
Marché St Pierre and turned the fashion world inside-out with
his fabulous rebellious designs.

In particular, two areas in the city are traditionally associated
with the textile industry: the Sentier in the 2nd arrondissement
and Montmartre's Marché St Pierre in the 18th.

FABRICS

Coton – Cotton

Laine/lainage – Wool

Maille – Knit

Tissu extensible – Stretch fabric

Velours – Velvet

Soie – Silk

Mousseline de soie – Chiffon

Viscose - Rayon

Polaire / molleton – Polar fleece

Tissus chemise – Shirting

Laine feutrée – Felted wool

Velours côtelé – Corduroy

Jersey – Jersey

Dentelle – Lace

Lin – Linen

tissé – Woven

Toile à matelas – Mattress drill

Cuir – Leather

Peaux – Hide

Doublure – Lining

Liberty – Any fabric with tiny flower prints.

Ask for Liberty of London for true Liberty fabric.

THE SENTIER

The Sentier fits neatly into a rectangle comprising Rue Bonne Nouvelle as its top edge, Rue Réaumur as its bottom with Rue Montmartre on the left (west) side and Boulevard de Sébastopol on the right (east) side.

Inside the Sentier, tiny streets run at odd angles, narrow passages connect several streets and hidden courtyards offer a moment of quiet refuge for residents. Essentially a wholesale area, many shops are not open to individual shoppers. Others have made retail sales their business by negotiating with haute couture design houses and their fabric suppliers to buy leftover luxury fabric to sell from Sentier warehouses. Waves of change are nothing new in the Sentier, throughout its history changes in fashion, mechanical inventions – the sewing machine – and the arrival of imported fabric in the 17th century, have all impacted on local businesses. Today every style is possible for savvy dressmakers who know where to find the outlets carrying luxury and unusual fabrics.

A FRENCHMAN INVENTED THE SEWING MACHINE

In the early 1830s Monsieur Barthélemy Thimonnier, a French tailor with an inventive mind developed a sewing machine in partnership with his engineer colleague, Monsieur Ferrand. It sewed well enough making a crochet-like chain stitch so he built a number of machines and set up a factory to make army uniforms. Realising this speedy machine would mean less hand-sewing work and a potential loss of income, the local tailors took exception to Thimonnier and his invention. With typical French zest, the angry tailors destroyed the machine-sewing factory. Diverted but not deterred, Thimonnier carried on developing and securing patents for his improved sewing machines, but his stitching machine never caught on beyond France. New machines invented by Americans Mr. Howe and Mr. Singer were patented in the mid-1800s and ultimately Singer became synonymous with sewing machines.

Thimonnier's sewing machines are housed in the wonderful collection of technological inventions and innovations on display at the Arts et Métiers Museum.

60 Rue Réaumur, 75003 Paris
Ph: 01 53 01 82 00
www.arts-et-metiers.net
Metro: Arts et Métiers or Réaumur-Sébastopol

TISSU MARKET

Franck Lellouche, the owner of this wholesale and retail fabric outlet in the heart of Sentier, recalls starting out in his father's business in the "crazy busy" 1980s when it was commonplace to buy and sell 10,000 metres of unfinished fabrics in a day. Now he sources small-volume, high-quality surplus fabric from luxury brands to retail directly from his warehouse.

Mr Lellouche doesn't like to disclose names, and the luxury industry is notoriously tight-lipped, but you'll find here on-trend, top-of-the-range fabrics from Italy and France and "technical fabrics" from Japan and Belgium. Tissu Market prides itself on this. The same fabrics seen on the runway can be found stacked, ready and waiting for discovery on Tissu Market's shelves.

Tissu Market has two warehouses side by side on Rue Sentier, both stocked full of exciting fabrics in every textile imaginable: cashmere, printed silks, pure wool fabrics from Italy, fine shirting, linens and the latest technical fabrics.

Clients include independent fashion design businesses, costume designers for film, theatre and opera houses, as well as individuals: fashion students, visiting fashionistas who come to stock up on modern and "edgy" fabrics and holidaying seamstresses from all over the world.

Most of the staff speak English, and don't be surprised if the person assisting you is a design or couture student from the nearby fashion school.

The staff readily provide fabric samples, you can buy as little as one metre of fabric and pay by credit card, cash (or cheque if you have a French bank account). Tissu Market offers a 10% discount to students and holders of the Tissu Market welcome card.

18 and 20 Rue Sentier, Paris 75002
Ph: 01 42 21 47 53
www.tissumarket.com
Open: 10am to 1pm and 2pm to 6pm Monday to Friday, 10am to 6pm Saturday
Metro: Sentier or Bonne Nouvelle

GENERAL DIFF

It's no surprise that people who have been to General Diff describe it as the Aladdin's cave of fabric, or even the Louvre of fabric. It really is stacked full of treasure for sewing enthusiasts, and fashion lovers who wish they could sew!

General Diff is not a large echoing warehouse, but a compact shop where Max, the owner, and his daughter Magali cram every inch of space with luxurious fabrics bought directly from haute couture textile suppliers, and the bustle of the Sentier district outside is momentarily subdued. Surrounded by silk and more silk; silk velvet, silk jersey, silk faille, organza, silk lamé, and satins and linens in just as many confections, it almost beats being front row at a Paris fashion week show.

Generously discounted prices are offered in each part of the store. The street-level shop includes a selection of beautiful bridal silks in pale romantic shades of cream and white, exquisite Calais lace, beaded laces, silk zips, ribbons and trims. Below in the basement, shoppers find discounted coupons: designer fabrics pre-cut in three-metre lengths. Even if you don't know exactly what to make, with three metres of irresistible fabric there are plenty of creative possibilities. On the top floor, Max and Magali guide their customers through the range of fine woollens, tweeds, more silks – there are eighty bridal silks alone, the latest leather-look satin from Italy, cashmere, impossibly soft woven vicuna, and much

more, to tempt serious dressmakers and motivate debutantes to perfect their skills.

With a father who's been in textile for more than forty years, Magali grew up with fabric; she knows the provenance of every piece in the shop, its fibre content and qualities, and with a grin she recounts which celebrity recently wore a garment made from a particular fabric. She keeps an inspiration file of clippings from glossy magazines to share with customers. This family offers a delightful personal service and a wonderland of fabric that shoppers only learn about by word of mouth. For customers who return home and wish they had bought more, or discover another tempting fabric on General Diff's website, Magali will send a sample and the fabric length cut to measure. Oh so tempting.

44 Rue de Cléry, Paris 75002
Ph: 01 42 33 05 28
www.generaldiff.com
Open: Monday to Thursday 9am to 6pm, Friday 9am to 6pm in summer and 9am to 4pm in winter.
Metro: Sentier or Bonne Nouvelle

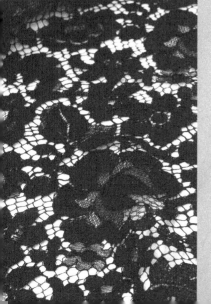

SILK

When your scissors rip through silk do you hear it scream? Can you tell true silk by the smell when it's burned? Do you love its lustre and smooth feel on bare skin? You are not alone. The love for silk has even inspired a movie. *The Cry of the Silk (Le Cri de la Soie)* – is a French film made in 1996 about a young seamstress with a fetish for the feel of silk. Set in 1914 Paris – great costumes and scenery – the young woman is arrested for attempting to steal silk from a department store. She is held in prison and interviewed by a psychiatrist who reveals his own weakness for the pleasure of textiles. Two passionate silk lovers; it's definitely a French film.

LES ETOFFES DU SENTIER

A warehouse on Rue des Jeuneurs, Les Etoffes du Sentier is typical of the district; the industrial space is neither beautiful nor elegant, not even shabby chic. Hefty bolts of fabric are stacked almost ceiling high, on the warehouse floor trolleys bearing more fabric wait to be unloaded and others wait to be loaded onto a delivery truck. Yet amid the bustle of business the hardworking staff offer eager sewists a friendly welcome at the coal face of the fabric trade and will happily shift bolts to find the right fabric, all the while relishing the chance to practise their English.

Les Etoffes du Sentier storage warehouse at number 5 Rue de Cléry is worth popping into if you are interested in leather. From time to time the storeroom tables are piled high with soft leather pieces in an impressive selection of colours and finishes. Endless rolls of fabric fill every alcove in this former factory whose industrial past is revealed by the wagon rails that cross the floor. Take great care if you venture into the basement as some stairs are broken.

At both Les Etoffes du Sentier warehouses a three-metre minimum cut rule applies (except for the leather pieces) and payment is by cash or cheque only, no credit cards.

12 Rue des Jeuneurs and 5 Rue de Cléry, Paris 75002

Open: Monday to Thursday 8.30am to 5.30pm, Friday 8.30am to 12.30, 2pm to 4.30pm

Metro: Sentier

SENTIER ADDRESSES TO STASH

In Rue de Mulhouse there are two fabric outlet stores that offer retail sales and are worth a visit. At Sonitis a three-metre minimum cut applies and they accept cash or French cheques, but no credit cards.

Sonitis, 11 Rue de Mulhouse, Paris 75002

Along the road at GHT Tissus, the minimum cut is one-metre.

GHT Tissus, 7 Rue de Mulhouse, Paris 75002

Metro: Sentier

Fil 2000

Popular sewing supply store, Fil 2000 on Rue Réaumur is a tiny shop where sewing professionals buy zips, buttons, thread and other notions. It's so popular yet compact that the queue often flows out the door.

65 Rue Réaumur, Paris 75002

Hamon

Since 1818, Hamon has supplied clothing workshops with tools and machines. Cast-iron replicas of the medals they won at the 1855 Universal Exhibition in Paris decorate the shop's exterior. For home-sewing needs they offer grading rulers, French curves, dressmakers' dummies, zips, pins, needles and best of all – scissors for every pocket of right-and left-handed crafters.

54 Rue de Cléry, Paris 75002

Ph: 01 42 33 27 59

www.hamon-paris.com

Open: Monday to Thursday 9am to 6pm, Friday 9am to 5pm

Metro: Bonne Nouvelle or Sentier

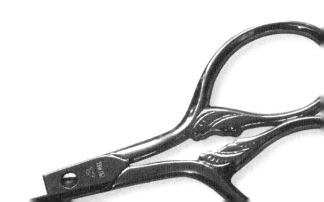

SCISSORS

The town of Nogent in the Champagne-Ardenne region is recognised for its fine scissors handmade by skilled craftsmen. Scissors bearing the Nogent mark are available in Paris at Hamon in the Sentier district and at the specialist cutting tools shop Courty & Fils on Rue des Petits Champs. Ask for *ciseaux lingère* for sewing scissors, *ciseaux à broder* for embroidery scissors, and *ciseaux tailleur* for tailor's shears. Look for the tiny marks on the inside of each blade. These tell you the scissors have a carefully matched pair of blades crafted only for each other. A marriage made in heaven.

Courty & Fils
44 Rue des Petits Champs, Paris 75002
Ph: 01 42 96 59 21
www.couteaux-courty.com
Metro: Pyramides or Opéra

NEIGHBOURHOOD NOTES

Here in the Sentier district a multitude of businesses related to the textile industry cluster around the fabric warehouses: dress form and mannequin vendors, scissor specialists, haberdashery and notions shops as well as the Esmod fashion school and *Mon Atelier en Ville*, creative workshop space where you can rent sewing machines by the hour.

The hubbub of activity starts early in the Sentier; while hip looking fashion students gather around the school door drawing the last puff on their cigarettes and café owners serve breakfast coffee at the counter, delivery trucks inch their way along old narrow streets – too narrow for door-to-door delivery. The only option is to stop mid-street, unload and ferry trolley loads of fabric down even narrower side streets. The job is done amid shouts, honking from jammed drivers and the incessant buzz of scooters whose riders deftly weave in and out and along the pavement to avoid the blockage.

Aboukir oasis

On the corner of Rue d'Aboukir and Rue des Petits Carreaux take a seat to admire the 25-metre-high vertical garden known as the Aboukir Oasis created from 7,600 plants fed by an automatic watering system. It is the work of renowned botanist and landscape designer, Patrick Blanc. Weeding and pruning requires a small crane.

La Penderie

The sewing-themed café La Penderie next to Etienne Marcel Metro station is a great spot to people watch while you enjoy coffee or a bite to eat.

17 Rue Etienne Marcel, Paris 75001
Open daily from 8am to 2am.

Itching to get stitching?

Check out the new workshop, Mon Atelier en Ville, at 30 Rue de Cléry. You can rent time on a sewing machine, serger or even a machine for sewing leather. They provide DIY tools, machinery and space for sewing, woodwork, sculpture, jewellery making, etc. This atelier is ideal for Parisians living in tiny apartments, and really energetic tourists who want to hand make their souvenirs before going home.

For further details:
www.monatelierenville.com
Phone: 09 82 55 08 34. English spoken.

Esmod

The fashion design school Esmod has its business section at 12 Rue de Cléry in the Sentier. In the lobby you can buy the school's bilingual Fr/Eng design and cutting books on draping, tailoring, pattern cutting, grading, lingerie and their well-known textiles guide. Just say *Bonjour* and point to the books as you pass the receptionist at the welcome desk.

www.esmod.com

MONTMARTRE FABRIC DISTRICT

Clustered at the foot of Montmartre below the Basilica Sacré Coeur and the old church of St Pierre, the fabric shops in this area are very well known, frequently written about by sewing bloggers and visited by tens of thousands of enthusiastic dressmakers every year.

The beginnings of St Pierre as a fabric district go back to the late 19th century when the Dreyfus and Moline families, cousins, routinely came to the cobbled streets at the foot of the Montmartre hill to sell fabrics off the back of their wagons. By the 1920s, the cousins set up fabric shops in large buildings in the neighbourhood and other fabric merchants followed.

This vibrant area is a bargain hunter's delight and requires shopping stamina. Be prepared to dig deep in the chaotic assortment of colours and textures that grab your attention from all directions. Some stores sell three-metre pre-cut lengths (coupons) only, others sell by the metre and by coupon.

DREYFUS MARCHÉ ST PIERRE

Standing before the prime-positioned Dreyfus Marché St Pierre, where Rue Charles Nodier, Rue Livingstone and Place St Pierre intersect, it's as if Emile Zola's 1883 novel *Au Bonheur des Dames (The Ladies' Delight)* describes this shop.

"There she saw, in the open street, on the very pavement, a mountain of cheap goods — bargains, placed there to tempt the passers-by, and attract attention. Hanging from above were pieces of woollen cloth goods, merinos, cheviots, and tweeds, floating like flags; the neutral, slate, navy-blue, and olive green tints being relieved by the large white price tickets. Close by, round the doorway were hanging strips of fur, narrow bands for dress trimmings, fine Siberian squirrel-skin, spotless snowy swansdown, rabbit-skin imitation ermine and imitation sable."

You won't find Siberian squirrel skin these days, but the volume of offerings hasn't changed. The enticement to buy begins on the pavement with the cheerful jumble of cut-price fabrics that overflow from bins. Venture inside for the best bargains on the ground floor and be sure to explore all five floors. It's worth climbing the stairs for a superb view of the Basilica Sacré Coeur from the midst of furnishing fabrics on level five, or take the lift and exchange *bonjours* with the friendly attendant as you ascend.

The entire shop, all 2,500 square metres, is stuffed with fabric, from cute printed cottons for children's wear, to flashy sequins and sparkles, novelty plastics, jersey and sweater knits, French Toile de Jouy cottons, linens, tartans, denim; it's all here even silks and satins and furnishing fabrics on the top floor. Dreyfus Marché St Pierre's draw card is price. At every price level there are bargains to be had; offering the best price is the company's mission.

Bargains mean business and the pace on the shop floors is often hectic. In the midst of swathes of fabric, floor managers like Mr Bob keep order. Shop floor staff are equipped and ready with a yard stick (or metre measure) and draper's scissors, reeling off chosen fabrics with a flourish and cutting to measure — anything from half a metre — before scribbling details on their colour coded sale dockets. At checkout, customers present the coloured dockets for the cashier to tally the bill. There's time for a quick conversation, a bit of laughter before the essential *Bonne journée* and the next customer is served. So well known now, Dreyfus Marché St Pierre attracts customers from all over the world, everyone enjoying the thrill of a bargain hunt, but it's all in a day's work for the industrious shop floor family, some of whom have worked here for more than 30 years and are third-generation employees.

2 Rue Charles Nodier, Paris 75018
Ph: 01 46 06 92 25
www.marchesaintpierre.com
Open: Monday to Friday 10am to 6.30pm; Saturday 10am to 7pm
Metro: Anvers or Abbesses

LE BON MARCHÉ INSPIRED ZOLA

Emile Zola's novel *Au Bonheur des Dames* was in fact inspired by Le Bon Marché department store on Rue de Sèvres in the elegant 7th arrondissement. Today it is Paris's most luxurious and refined department store, selling almost everything from fresh mouth-watering food in the gourmet grocery store, to fine home wares, furniture, designer handbags, shoes and fabulous clothing. They no longer sell fabric and knitting yarn — or Siberian squirrel-skin.

24 Rue de Sèvres, Paris 75007
Open: Monday to Saturday 10am to 8pm
Metro: Sèvres-Babylone

TOILE DE JOUY

Toile de Jouy is the name given to cotton fabric printed with images of people in bucolic settings. This type of printed fabric was manufactured by French entrepreneur Christophe-Philippe Oberkampf at a factory he established in 1760 at Jouy en Josas not far from Paris.

One hundred years before, when the bright-printed cottons called *les Indiennes* were first imported to France by the Compagnie des Indes they quickly became very popular; too popular for French silk manufacturers whose profits were threatened. As a result, *les Indiennes* were banned in France from 1686 to 1759 in order to protect the local textile industry. Banning proved futile as demand for the fashionable prints simply grew.

For a wonderful day trip out of Paris visit the Toile de Jouy museum, tea and gift shop in the Château Eglantine at Jouy en Josas. There is an excellent collection of printed textiles, fabric printing equipment, drawings and designs.

Open: Tuesday to Sunday 11am to 6pm, for details see:
www.museedelatoiledejouy.fr/en-GB/index.aspx

TISSUS REINE

If Dreyfus is the king, then the queen of the Marché St Pierre area is Tissus Reine, which offers shoppers a more refined atmosphere befitting the heritage of the Bouchara fabric family. Established in 1930 and named after Monsieur Bouchara's daughter, Reine, this store takes shoppers back to a time when every large town throughout the world had a fabric store just like this.

Hundreds of rolls of quality fabrics are laid out for browsing shoppers to touch, match colours and visualise creations before purchasing. For generations of French sewists the dressed-up, doll-sized mannequins standing above the fabric tables bring back memories of the beloved Bouchara fabric store that occupied prime position on Boulevard Haussmann. On the next floor an immense selection of notions and finishings makes Tissus Reine a welcome one-stop-shop for busy Parisian sewists especially as the ever-popular patterns *Vogue, Simplicity, McCall's, Butterick* and *Burda* are still to be found in the now-rare pattern department, (closed on Wednesdays and Thursdays). On the floor above, rolls and rolls of elegant furnishing fabrics, striped mattress ticking and household linens offer do-it-yourself decorators an infinite choice of style and colour scheme.

5 Place St Pierre, Paris 75018
Ph: 01 46 06 02 31
Open: Tuesday to Saturday 9.30am to 6.30 pm, and Monday 2pm to 6.30pm.
www.tissus-reine.com
Metro: Anvers or Abbesses

SACRÉS COUPONS

The bright blue-and-white-striped awnings make Sacrés Coupons stores easy to pick out along the row of similarly named stores that line Rue d'Orsel and adjacent streets. As the name suggests, the fabrics here are sold as coupons – three-metre pre-cut lengths – and there is a grand selection.

Sacrés Coupons' two stores, side by side, are favoured destinations for the international community of sewing bloggers, it is not uncommon to overhear conversations in several languages and don't be surprised if you bump into someone you've read online. In the larger store, alongside silks, woollens and cottons are bright swimwear textiles, unusual high-tech fabrics for raincoats such as double-sided neoprene, while next door a large selection of skins, fake fur, boiled wool and knit fabrics await creative couturiers. If the shop is not busy a kind staff member may agree to cut a coupon in half for you, provided it is not the last one.

Sacrés Coupons' best-kept secret: their outlet store for extra bargains is tucked away on tiny Rue Seveste, worth a look.

4 bis Rue d'Orsel, Paris 75018
Ph: 01 42 64 69 96
www.sacrescoupons.fr
Open: Monday to Saturday 9.30am to 7pm.
Metro: Anvers or Abbesses

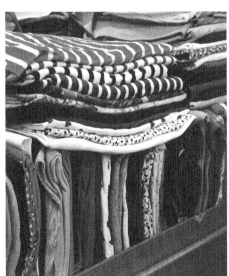

MONTMARTRE FABRIC DISTRICT
ADDRESSES TO STASH

Large and small fabric outlets operate cheek by jowl along Place St Pierre, Rue Charles Nodier, into Rue Livingstone and Rue d'Orsel. The quiet side streets Rue Seveste and Rue Pierre Picard have bargain basement stores while in Rue André del Sarte trendy new fashion shops pop up to entice.

Frou-Frou Mercerie Contemporaine

Across the road from Moline, this store was originally Moline's haberdashery department. It has been modernised and renamed as part of the Frou-Frou Mercerie Contemporaine family of retail outlets. The Frou-Frou business is known for its pretty and conveniently packaged notions: ribbons, buttons, laces, edgings and fabrics including iron-on fabric shapes.

2, 4 and 6 Rue Livingstone, Paris 75018
www.frou-frou-mercerie-contemporaine.com
Open: Monday to Saturday 10am to 7pm.

Tissu Market

The carefully arranged rows of stylish fabrics protectively tied with cotton tape in this little store state emphatically that this place is neither a warehouse nor a jumble sale. The sight gives textile lovers pleasure knowing these beauties are well looked after. This store, although not identified on the company's website, is a branch of Tissu Market in the Sentier and definitely merits a visit to peruse the collection of exclusive fabrics that have likely graced the pages of a glossy fashion magazine.

25 Rue d'Orsel, Paris 75018
Open: Monday to Saturday 10am to 6pm, closed for lunch 1pm to 2pm

NEIGHBOURHOOD NOTES

Rue Ronsard and Rue Charles Nodier

After the hustle and bustle of the big busy fabric stores wander along to the peaceful end of Rue Ronsard to restore the sense of calm. In the window of the old fashioned upholstery shop halfway along the street a haphazard collection of antique chair frames, fabrics and ornaments contrasts unintentionally with the chic understated elegance of the window displays at Karin Sajo's furnishing fabric showroom next door. Her stylish showroom fronts onto a gorgeous square, perfect for snapping a few holiday photos.

Karin Sajo, 3 Rue Charles Nodier,
Paris 75018

www.karinsajo.com

Opposite the square the steep tree-lined steps lead up the hill to Sacré Coeur. On Rue André del Sarte, the café No Problemo offers a quiet vantage point, or stroll further to the friendly Le Café du Commerce on the corner of Rue Pierre Picard and Rue Clignancourt.

If, between them, the Sentier and Marché St Pierre districts claim the honour of being the most concentrated fabric districts in Paris, then addresses elsewhere in the city are like precious jewels that add sparkle and interest. Parisians know to value a distant shop that offers quality pieces.

K H AFRIQUE MODE

Explore Boulevard Barbès to find the pulse of modern multicultural Paris. It's not a typical tourist route, but you can detour to discover vivid African-printed wax fabrics at K H Afrique Mode on Rue Doudeauville off Boulevard Barbès.

Masses of top-quality Vlisco fabrics in exotic motifs are stacked in well-organised piles on the display counters and decorate the walls in kaleidoscopic glory. All fabric is sold in pre-cut six-yard lengths, never less.

77 Rue Doudeauville, Paris 75018
Ph: 01 42 59 08 49
Open: Monday to Saturday 10am to 8pm.
Email: k.h.afrique-mode@hotmail.com
(in French)
Metro: Château-Rouge

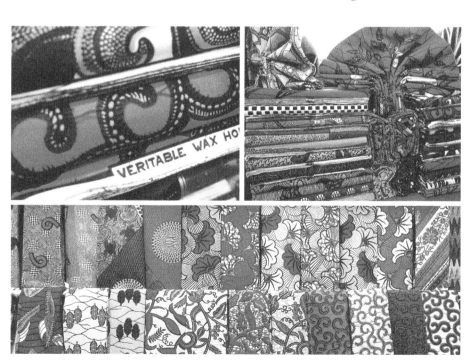

MALHIA KENT

Malhia Kent's textile and thread outlet store on the inspirational Viaduc des Arts route is a place where adventurous creativity is cultivated. It is a fabric-and-fibre fantasyland for daring dressmakers, audacious knitters and crocheters on the edge who push the boundaries to experiment and have fun with crafting. Boucle, mohair, wool and sparkly metallic threads line the wooden shelves; bright neon tape and glittering sequins trail from their cones as if trying to escape into a new project.

Malhia Kent is a French fabric design house known for its eye-catching woven textiles made from European-sourced threads. Striking sample fabrics are hand-woven for fashion design houses, often in collaboration with the clothing designers themselves. Fabric samples that do not progress to commercial manufacture, leftover fabrics from production runs and cones of thread used in manufacturing are all sold here at discount prices.

The cones of thread are sold "as is" for the whole cone; prices marked but usually with little information as to fibre content. Savvy crafters who know their fibres, or who like to take a chance, can pick up a few hundred grams or even a kilo of colour and sparkle for a few euros. Fabrics are sold in variable pre-cut lengths and priced accordingly, while the minimum length sold from the bolts of fabric is fifty centimetres.

Viaduc des Arts, 19 Avenue Daumesnil, Paris 75012
Ph: 01 53 44 78 75
www.malhia.fr
Open: Tuesday to Friday 10am to 2pm, 3pm to 7pm. Saturday 11am to 2pm, 3pm to 7pm.
Metro: Bastille, Ledru-Rollin or Gare de Lyon

NEIGHBOURHOOD NOTES

The genteel Passy neighbourhood offers a covered market on Place de Passy open every day except Monday, starting at 8am and closing at 1pm before opening again late afternoon (except on Sundays when it stays closed). Rue de l'Annonciation is a pedestrian-only street filled with boutiques perfectly suited for a leisurely stroll and window shopping: chocolatiers, butchers – including one with a parking space for dogs – a specialist cheesemonger, a caviar shop, greengrocers and a florist, a depôt-vente and an antique store await exploration.

For elegant high street shopping stroll along Rue de Passy and browse fashion stores without the crowds of the tourist zones. The very chic Franck et Fils department store at number 80, originally a *mercerie* established by Madame Franck in 1897 and expanded by her son to become a department store, is now part of the Bon Marché group offering luxury brands in a refined atmosphere and delectable refreshments at the in-store café.

Musée Marmottan Monet

From La Muette metro stop a 10-minute walk through Jardin de Ranelagh brings colour devotees to Passy's elegant Musée Marmottan Monet. A superb collection of Impressionist works by Claude Monet – including his painting of the sun rising that gave the name to impressionism – Berthe Morisot and their artist contemporaries grace the walls of this old hunting lodge. Enjoy the privilege of strolling through the former private home of a wealthy art collector, bask in Monet's dreamy cascading willows over water lilies, Morisot's cherished family scenes and catch the latest special exhibition.

2 Rue Louis Boilly, Paris 75016
Open: daily, except Mondays,
10am to 6pm. Thursdays 10am to 9pm.
www.marmottan.fr
Metro: La Muette

SEVILLA

Tucked in beside a lively Passy neighbourhood greengrocer this shop illustrates the old adage that good things come in small packages. It might not be a tidy package, but it is packed full of good haute couture fabrics from the design houses and their suppliers' surplus stock.

What you see is what you can get; labels announcing Prada and Yves Saint Laurent swing from the material, while Hermès and Givenchy are noted in plain writing on the spine of the bolt and the last length is the last, snap up what you see or miss out.

Sevilla has been around since the early sixties when Mr Sevilla's father ran the business, canny Parisian dressmakers still keep it on their bargain watch list.

38 Rue de l'Annonciation, 75016 Paris
Ph: 01 42 88 11 13
Open: Tuesday 9.30am to 12.45, Wednesday to Saturday 9.30am to 12.45 and 3pm to 6.30pm.
Metro: La Muette

FRANCE DUVAL STALLA

France Duval Stalla courageously started her own fabric design business simply because she couldn't find the type of fabric she wanted to sew for her three young children – good quality fabric printed with modern designs and sold by the metre. Her sense of style and eye for quality is confirmed by her popularity with her fabrics now available at several boutiques in Paris (including Brin de Cousette, Les Petits Points Parisiens, L'Atelier and Lil Weasel).

Her left-bank showroom exudes an air of youthful pizzazz that matches her own vitality and energy. Bright-coloured quilted knit material awaits active toddlers, woven baskets overflow with tempting fabric remnants. The latest fabrics from favourite contemporary textile designers Nani Iro, Atelier Brunette, Linna Morata and Liberty make this address a welcome stop for a new generation of enthusiastic Parisian sewists, young mothers and sewing bloggers.

24 Rue Mayet, Paris 75006
Ph: 09 50 43 50 10
Open: Tuesday, Thursday, Friday and Saturday 10.30am to 7pm, Monday 10.30am to 4pm. Closed Wednesday and Sunday.
www.franceduvalstalla.com
Metro: Duroc or Falguière

INÈS PATCHWORK

With masses of fabric squares picked ready-mitered some hours (we're in France after all) and row upon row of carefully folded fabrics on shelves this shop is a tempting destination for patchwork enthusiasts.

Alongside the patterned fabrics from all over the world, which may be familiar to well-travelled patchworkers, there are traditional Toile de Jouy prints in faded rustic tones and colourful Provençal prints. Christiane Boudouani has been retailing patchwork supplies for more than twenty years; she and her team know what their clients like and fill the shop with everything required, even offering classes for beginners and particular projects. Having helped many novice patchworkers choose fabrics, cut pieces and stitch their first works of art she has put together a ready-to-stitch kit for those who want to try their hand at patchwork.

37 Rue Saint-Ambroise, Paris 75011
Ph: 01 43 38 54 86
www.inespatchwork.com
Open: Tuesday to Saturday
10.30am to 6.30pm.
Metro: Saint-Ambroise or Rue Saint-Maur

BRIN DE COUSETTE – THE SEWING CAFÉ

Pause for a while; fill the well of sewing inspiration at Brin de Cousette. The owners, Morgann and Aissatou, established their lovely little sewing café for this very reason. The two long-time friends and sewing buddies believed that while Paris had plenty of great fabric stores there was a need for a place where sewing debutantes and proficient dressmakers alike could talk and share their passion for fabric and all things sewing. They percolated on the idea a while longer until the right moment arrived in 2012 to launch their venture.

Inside the cosy café, display space is filled with fun sewing notions, an expanding range of modern designer fabrics including France Duval Stalla, Atelier Brunette, Soft Cactus, as well as certified organic brands Lillestoff and Les Trouvailles d'Amandine. They offer sought-after indie sewing patterns by Tilly and the Buttons, Papercut, Deer and Doe, By Hand, Colette, Lila Fait des Bulles, Coupe Cousu, Pauline Alice, République de Chiffon and, for men's clothing, Thread Theory. The ever-popular *Burda* and *Ottobre* sewing magazines are for sale, or you can browse the shop's copy over tea or coffee. Knitting and sewing classes can be booked online.

The comprehensive à la carte classes cater to beginners and accomplished sewists looking to experiment. Outside of class time, the machines are available for hourly hire and the workshop space multitasks for business team building sessions or even a bridal shower party.

2 Rue Richard Lenoir, Paris 75011
Ph: 01 43 72 58 09
www.brindecousette.com
Book a class
Open: Tuesday 12.30pm to 7pm; Wednesday to Saturday, 10am to 7pm
Metro: Voltaire or Faidherbe-Chaligny

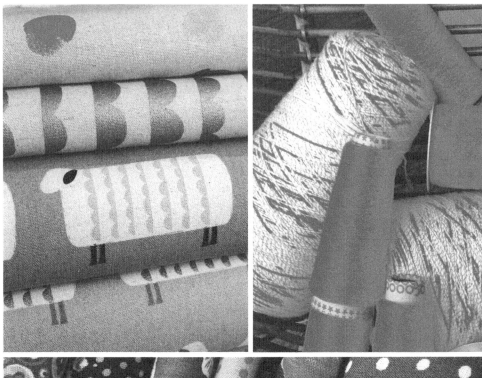

ADDRESSES TO STASH

IE

128 Rue Vieille de Temple, Paris 75003
Ph: 01 44 59 87 72
www.ieboutique.com
Open: Monday 1pm to 7pm; Tues to Sunday 11am to 7pm
Metro: Filles du Calvaire or Saint-Sébastien-Froissart

For pretty cotton fabric in amusing and dainty prints, sold by the metre from 50cm minimum.

Petit Pan St Paul

76 Rue François Miron, Paris 75004
www.petitpan.com
Open: Monday and Sunday: 10.30am to 2pm and 3pm to 7.30pm, Tuesday to Saturday: 10.30am to 7.30pm
Metro: Saint-Paul

The Petit Pan boutiques offer a contemporary range of coordinated fabrics and sewing notions: 100% cottons, plasticised fabric, quilted fabric, patchwork squares and trims, all in colourful matching designs. Branches exist in Toulouse and Belgium.

"*Embroidery is a craft using simply a needle and thread, but with exacting skill artists create pieces of beauty and historic importance.*"

EMBROIDERY

Needle and thread has been used to decorate cloth for centuries. Techniques for hand stitching have barely changed over time – which is part of the appeal. Embroidery is a craft using simply a needle and thread, but with exacting skill artists create pieces of beauty and historic importance.

Embroidery is practised by skilled artisans, by amateurs and in families where the skills are passed down through generations. In previous eras it was taught in schools along with academic subjects, and in the Middle Ages it was virtually the only education provided for young women. In the sixties, the practice fell out of vogue as unfitting for liberated women, and digital industrialisation diluted its exclusivity. But embroidery survives zeitgeist and societal turmoil; millions of embroiderers still enjoy the pleasure of hand crafting everything from works of art to practical everyday items with needle and thread.

ANNIE BOUQUET'S TAPISSERIE DE FRANCE

Even before the needlework begins on an heirloom project such as a tapestry-covered Louis-XV cabriolet armchair, many hours of Annie Bouquet's artisan skills have gone into designing, drawing and painting the canvas template. Each handcrafted design from her atelier is presented for sale in a kit comprising the painted canvas ready for needlework together with exactly the right quantity of high quality woollen or silk thread in colours expertly matched to the original painted canvas, a tapestry needle, written stitching instructions, historical notes, and when required a graphic template for the tapestry border.

Annie trained as a graphic artist before migrating into fabric art and tapestry design, eventually setting up her own specialty tapestry design workshop in 1978. Her design store is located in central Paris near the Palais Garnier Opera House. The shop's interior brims with beautiful tapestry cushions, wall hangings and furniture; antique chairs and footstools, along with small novelty projects – spectacle and phone cases, pin cushions, brooches and hair clasps – to inspire stitchers whose ambitions don't (yet) extend that far.

Her designs stem from historical art and interior decor styles, which she cleverly adapts for smaller projects. Among the 2000 designs in her catalogue is a series of fourteen canvases depicting playful monkeys inspired by the 18th century Christophe Huet wall panels at Château Chantilly near Paris. Annie initially made

six paintings, a client then requested six more, and eventually another two to complete a large wall hanging. Annie paints classical designs based on the famous *Lady and the Unicorn* tapestries and also vibrant modern designs to suit contemporary interiors. When customers commission an original design, perhaps to cover an antique chair or footstool, Annie uses her knowledge of art and interior design history to create the canvases in a period style harmonious with the furniture it will decorate and the room in which it will reside.

7 Rue des Moulins, Paris 75001
Ph: 01 42 60 65 67
www.tapisseriedefrance.fr
Open: Monday and Saturday 2 to 7pm;
Tuesday to Friday 10am to 7pm
Metro: Pyramides or Quatre-Septembre

EMBROIDERY AND WOMEN'S LIBERATION

In the early 1980s, Monique Lyonnet and another passionate needlewoman Laurence Roque joined forces to establish a needlework boutique on Rue Saint-Martin in central Paris. Monique recalls that people initially disparaged the idea: practising needlework, let alone enjoying it, wasn't for modern free-thinking women. However, in 1986 two feisty and famous French women writers, Régine Deforges and Geneviève Dormann, appeared on the popular Apostrophe show hosted by Bernard Pivot on French national television. Alongside Nobel-prize winning authors on the same episode, the two women stitched away on their needlework projects while discussing their recently published book (Le Livre du Point de Croix). Monique said that suddenly opinions reversed: these two women demonstrated that needlework was for liberated, influential career women after all.

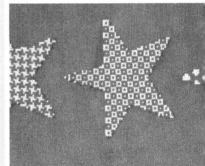

LA CROIX ET LA MANIÈRE

Madame Monique Lyonnet's needlecraft boutique, La Croix et La Manière on Rue Faidherbe in the 11th arrondissement is the epitome of understated elegance. The embroidery linens, threads and notions are artistically set out in a tasteful modern style dispelling any thought that embroidery might be a stuffy out-dated pastime.

Attractive fabrics and embroidery threads blend harmoniously with household linens displayed on the old wooden shelves of what was once the local appliance repair shop. Monique liked the good bones of the old workshop and used her skills in interior architecture, needlework and retailing to transform the space into a showcase for embroidery projects made with the materials available to buy in her shop.

It's no coincidence that the clean simple look of the boutique evokes the ambience of Danish design. It is a style that captured Monique when she was given a Danish needlework kit many years ago and immediately started on the path of self-taught embroidery. She has since published several embroidery design books, which are available in her shop, as is the beautiful Parisian cross-stitch design book *Rues de Paris* by Anne Sohier Fournel.

All fabrics, threads, trims and embellishments are sourced from small artisanal companies that produce high-quality materials. Tea towels, which can be embroidered with personalised designs, are woven in Belgium and Northern France, and sewing fabrics are sourced from Austria. Knitting yarns from the French company Fonty have been added to the range in sympathetic colours to coordinate with fabrics and thread.

La Croix et La Manière offers needlework classes, knitting classes and advice. Monique's design ideas encompass gifts for children and adults, home wares and even mini-kits to embroider personalised designs onto perforated gift card.

36 Rue Faidherbe, Paris 75011
Ph: 01 43 72 99 09
www.lacroixetlamaniere.com
Open: Tuesday to Saturday noon to 7pm
Metro: Charonne or Faidherbe-Chaligny

THE CLUNY MUSEUM – NATIONAL MUSEUM OF THE MIDDLE AGES

The six historic tapestries of *the Lady and the Unicorn* series are displayed in a newly renovated space at the Cluny Museum in the Latin Quarter. The rich compositions and meticulous detail in these magnificent tapestries create a dramatic impression; highly recommended.

6 Place Paul-Painlevé, Paris 75005
www.musee-moyenage.fr
Open: Every day (except Tuesday) 9.15am to 5.45pm
Metro: Cluny-La Sorbonne, Saint-Michel or Odéon

NEIGHBOURHOOD NOTES

La Promenade Plantée and Viaduct des Arts

The Planted Promenade extends 4.5 km eastward from Place de la Bastille to the Bois de Vincennes and includes playground spaces, a few tunnels and trench-like gullies. It was created in 1988 as part of the Paris city project to rejuvenate the derelict Bastille to Varenne-Saint Maur railway line by planting a walkway and converting the space below to galleries and creative workshops. Along the promenade are cherry trees, roses, lavender and green bamboo corridors while in springtime this elevated garden offers some of the earliest daffodils. Accessed via staircases and lifts at intervals along Avenue Daumesnil, it takes you one level above the street noise and bustle.

LE BONHEUR DES DAMES

The artistic Viaduct des Arts provides a lofty space for Le Bonheur des Dames embroidery shop. The space was one of the galleries developed as a Paris renovation project to convert an old railway viaduct into retail stores, galleries and workshops for creative artisans.

Here under the arch you'll find a light airy gallery displaying hundreds of founder Cécile Vessière's cross-stitch designs. The shop stocks an immense range of cross stitch and embroidery kits from the Bonheur des Dames catalogue as well as other popular cross stitch brands, haberdashery, embroidery fabrics, gifts, books, patchwork fabrics and fat squares.

From the ever-popular ABC samplers to new design series featuring Russian dolls, owls, cats or chickens there are kits in all styles, sizes and complexities to suit every skill level, including kits for children. Every step in the production of the kits is done in-house from design to assembly and packaging of the kits complete with charts, threads and fabric. Madame Vessière is still creating new designs, while her son has taken over running the business.

For a petite-size version of Le Bonheur des Dames boutique visit the historic Passage Verdeau in the 9th arrondissement. Comfortably tucked away beside antique book and curiosity stores, art galleries and graceful tea salons, the sister shop stocks the same excellent merchandise – albeit in smaller quantity – and the setting cries out for you to snap some photos.

17 Avenue Daumesnil, Paris 75012
Ph: 01 43 42 06 27
Open: Monday to Saturday 10.30am to 7pm
Metro: Bastille, Ledru-Rollin or Gare de Lyon

8 Passage Verdeau, Paris 75009
Ph: 01 45 23 06 11
www.bonheurdesdames.com
Open: Monday 11.30am to 7pm, Tuesday to Saturday 10.30am to 7pm, with daily closing 2 to 2.30pm for lunch break.
Metro: Richelieu-Drouot

LES BRODEUSES PARISIENNES

A delightful boutique for embroidery enthusiasts located in the bohemian 11th arrondissement. The window display first captures your eye and tempts you inside where pretty things abound and an atmosphere of genteel femininity makes browsing and choosing a delight.

Les Brodeuses Parisiennes offers top quality ready-to-embroider linen tea towels, pretty purses and cotton project bags with blank linen or aida panels. The bags and purses are expertly sewn in France and finished in a way to allow a choice of embroidery design with one of the delightful templates or you can customise the design to suit your style, skill and threads available in your stash. Cute sewing projects for children, trendy notions, threads and haberdashery goods make ideal souvenir gifts.

New embroidery designs are released frequently. These include traditional flower and fruit motifs, modern "pop" style where embroidery designs are combined with pretty spotted fabric, vintage style with a mod twist, special seasonal projects and designs especially for beginners.

The owners, Judith and Sophie, are the creative minds behind the designs; they work closely with pattern drafters and their fabric manufacturers, cleverly incorporating the latest trends into their designs. They have both been involved in the world of embroidery for many years having established their careers as editors of leading cross stitch publications. When they launched Les Brodeuses Parisiennes' on-line store the response on social media and blogging circles was overwhelming and their web designer declared embroiderers to be mad! No just passionate like us, they cheered.

Now their boutique serves as their design workshop and is open three afternoons per week: Wednesday to Friday plus two Saturdays each month. They regularly exhibit at major European craft fairs.

---

1 Rue François de Neufchâteau, Paris 75011
Ph: 01 40 24 20 80
www.lesbrodeusesparisiennes.com
Open: Wednesday to Friday 1pm to 6pm. Check website for monthly Saturday opening days.
Metro: Charonne or Voltaire

PARIS CRAFT FAIRS

The two major craft fairs held at the Parc des Expositions in Paris are red-letter events for stitchers and stashers.

Aiguille en fête

A four-day event held every year in early February, Aiguille en Fête is the premier salon for creative activities involving needlework, fabric, yarn and stitching of any type. In 2015 there were over 250 retail exhibitors from around the world offering all manner of fabric, yarn, thread, books, materials, machines and notions to boot. It is an opportunity to meet retailers who normally sell online only, and many established boutiques use the occasion of Aiguille en Fête to launch new merchandise, pattern designs, fabric, yarn and colour ranges at their stand.

In addition to being a magnificent shopping experience to build up your stash, there is an excellent choice of masterclasses, ateliers, workshops and demonstrations across the needle arts. Each year the salon organisers choose a theme for a creative art exhibition showing leading works from some of the world's most talented fibre and textile artists.

For full information visit **www.aiguille-en-fete.com**

Créations et Savoir-Faire – Make it Yourself

This fair, sponsored by Marie Claire Idées magazine, takes place toward the end of November each year, usually running from Wednesday to Sunday. It caters to all types of creative hobbies from stitching and needlecraft to cooking, scrapbooking, painting, furniture decoration, jewellery making, cake decoration and more. Promoted as the Number 1 Make-it-Yourself fair in Paris, workshops, demonstrations, and an immense variety of activities are scheduled to keep you busy over the 5-day event.

For full information visit **www.creations-savoir-faire.com**

Both fairs are very popular and jam-packed at peak attendance times from late morning to mid afternoon and on the weekends. The Parc des Expositions at Porte de Versailles is easily accessible by public transport.

Metro: Porte de Versailles

"These magical stores lure in crafters the way sweet shops attract six year olds."

HABERDASHERY, NOTIONS AND PASSEMENTERIE

We needlecrafters might know them by different names: haberdashery, *mercerie* or notions stores, but the fascination is universal. Full of trinkets and baubles, buttons and threads, nifty things we need – and some that we don't – these magical stores lure in crafters the way sweet shops attract six year olds. Passementerie covers a broad collection of ornamental thread decorations such as tassels, edgings, fringes, braid and trim, twisted cords and pompoms.

ULTRAMOD

Popping out of the Metro at Quatre-Septembre stop and strolling just a short way along the street toward Passage Choiseul in search of Ultramod you might be a little taken aback. From the outside, ultra-mod doesn't seem quite the word to describe the pair of shops facing each other on either side of Rue de Choiseul.

In the window of the general mercerie store an array of vintage scissors and knitting needles, some cotton reels, pins and thread give an inkling of the array of notions to be found inside, while on the opposite side of the street the hats and tulle and trim are obvious clues to its specialty. The slightly shabby appearance though is all part of the charm of Ultramod.

Among buttons, ribbons, petersham, silk flowers, and lace still available from by-gone days when gentlemen carried canes and hats were a fashion necessity there is a selection of beautiful Duchesse satin in colours as delicate as the creatures they are named after. *Tourterelle, biche,* and *isard* (dove, doe and chamois) are the favourites for Marc the manager, or Monsieur Marc as he's amiably called on the shop floor.

The hat and furnishing shop opposite could be mistaken for a fashion archive with shelves stacked full of passementerie: trims, tassels, bobbles and braids in gorgeous colour combinations that costume designers drool over. Mr Marc, formerly a costume maker for an amateur dance group, has a magic touch when it comes to making and embellishing hats. He gathers up a length of bias sinamay, wraps and twists the fabric and *voilà!* the

beginnings of a gorgeous hat materialise. There's plenty more to beguile hat-makers; felt hoods made from hare fur for cloches, pillboxes and fedoras, and straw, sisal, singalette or raffia hat bases, netting and veiling for capelines, half hats, turbans and fascinators.

Delightful staff, enchanting surroundings and extraordinary notions cast a powerful spell. Enjoy the charm, it lasts as long as the grosgrain ribbons from the 1930s and 1940s that completely cover the counter in Mr Marc's hat making domain.

Ultramod is not just a tourist destination; all the modern notions needed for hand crafts sit comfortably alongside the traditional haberdashery stockpiled from the original shop. Faithful clients return again and again, while new customers, children and teenagers with creative aspirations, persuade their parents to visit and buy the goods they need.

3 and 4 Rue de Choiseul, Paris 75002
Ph: 01 42 96 98 30
www.ultramod-paris.com/boutique/fr
Open: Monday to Friday 10am to 6pm
Metro: Quatre-Septembre

DAM BOUTONS

Close your eyes, imagine yourself surrounded by 20,000 different buttons in every colour, size and texture possible; mirrored buttons, fabric, crystal, ceramic, even fur. Now open your eyes and find yourself in button heaven: Dam Boutons.

Around the corner from the bustling Marché St Pierre fabric area, those in the know flock to this little boutique at the quiet end of Rue d'Orsel. It's rumoured that haute couture designers shop here and well-to-do Parisiennes drop by in chauffeured limousines to select buttons. But the owner, Marianne, is discreet; a charming smile is the only acknowledgement, she won't unbutton her lips about her famous clients.

Marianne's greatest love, apart from Nanou her cute-as-a-button little Parisian pooch, is helping her clients select the perfect buttons for their project. She's emphatic: please ask for help if you need it. For Marianne, buttons are the jewels of clothing, veritable objets d'art, and with so many to choose from, her wise counsel is invaluable.

Working in haute couture she learnt to appreciate the magic of the right button, then starting her own business with just a small selection of buttons to complement fabrics Marianne couldn't resist adding more beauty, and fifteen years on, she is a button specialist.

There are buttons here to suit every style from elegant pink knots edged in gold to adorn a Chanel-styled suit to edgy modern-art pieces, and sweet little buttons to make a child's garment a favourite. Every other type of fastener is available too: Frog closures, buckles, domes, pins for turning buttons into brooches and charms for bracelets.

As bloggers and fashion magazines spread the word about the variety at Dam Boutons, followers from all over the world come to browse the thousands of exquisite buttons. With such a vast array it's understandable that Marianne has instituted a polite house-rule not to completely remove the button tubes from their carefully determined places in the shelves, just leave your favourites jutting out ready for the final choice.

Marianne's artistic flair extends beyond buttons; she delights in embroidery, designing and making stained glass pieces and painting.

46 Rue d'Orsel, Paris 75018
Ph: 01 53 28 19 51
www.damboutons.com
Open: Monday 1.30pm to 6.30pm, Tuesday to Saturday 10.30am to 1pm, 1.30pm to 6.30pm
Metro: Anvers

BAEYENS

This old-fashioned family-run workshop offers accessories for leather craft and travel bags plus everything for finishing handmade fabric, leather, knitted or crochet bags. Located in an unremarkable residential street, Rue des Trois Couronnes in the 11th arrondissement, it won't appear on any tourist map, but it is an amazing place to go for the necessary accessories to close, zip up, lock or fasten your trendy handmade bags.

Madame Baeyens still runs the business that her husband opened in 1941. She remembers as a teenager visiting her aunt's fish shop where, next door, young Monsieur Baeyens had set up shop. They married once the Second World War ended and navigated the changes brought by new locking mechanisms to shut shopping bags and hand bags. The arrival of the backpack as a fashion item allowed them to carry a whole new array of straps, buckles and fasteners.

Madame Baeyens is not only familiar with every button, rivet and snap lock on site; she has a wealth of knowledge and experience. Whatever her clients need, she offers wise advice on the best way to use magnetic snaps, swivel snap hooks, swivel clips, twist locks, buckles, strap adjustors, clasps of every kind, rivets, d-rings and corner protectors. Madame Baeyens values quality and proudly details the precise manufacturing standards of her Swiss, German and Italian suppliers.

Whether you need something from a bygone fashion era for reviving a precious vintage purse, or something snappy and modern, you can bet this shop will be a good place to find it.

2 Rue des Trois Couronnes, Paris 75011
Ph: 01 43 57 43 85
Open: Monday to Friday 9.30am to 1pm
Metro: Couronnes or Parmentier

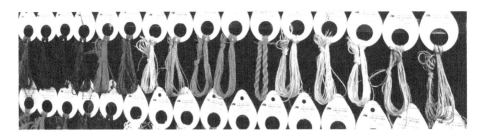

AU VER À SOIE

Au Ver à Soie – "the silk worm" – is a respected French family business that makes lustrous silk embroidery thread and ribbon, fine silk threads for sewing and silk fishing line and fly-tying threads. Au Ver à Soie has been based in the Sentier district since 1820 when the family established a silk spinning business.

Upstairs in an elegant stone building on Rue Réaumur, natural light bathes the showroom. All around the room silk threads attract the eye; pretty pinks and greens gleam from Soie de Paris shade cards, hundreds of reels of Soie Surfine cascade in subtle shifts of colour and on the shelves silk ribbons peep from tiny boxes.

Nathalie Boucher-Botherel opens the showroom to the public for an evening every February during the annual Paris stitching and craft fair, Aiguille-en-Fête, as well as for regular embroidery classes in Glazig techniques with effervescent embroidery artist and designer Pascal Jaouen from Brittany and for monthly embroidery workshops co-hosted with Parisian embroidery boutique, Atelier 196.

Nathalie, and her brother Marc, are the fifth continuous generation of Bouchers to run the company and they feel a profound sense of pride and responsibility to see it flourish in the 21st century. Over the years, the Boucher family has shown resilience and courage to overcome difficulties with sons killed in World War I, the factory destroyed by bombing raids in World War II and a fire that very recently gutted the present-day factory in the Loire Valley.

Feeling buoyed by the good wishes of customers from all over the world, and particularly touched by a card from an embroidery club in the US, the family is rebuilding and equipping the factory to ensure the longevity of the company for years to come.

Au Ver à Soie threads are used by haute couture houses, luxury garment and leather ware makers, jewellers and the healthcare industry. Au Ver à Soie threads, ribbons and kits are available through retailers in Paris and around the world. At present their products can be purchased directly from the showroom only during embroidery classes, at open evenings, and by arrangement during *Stitching up Paris* tours.

102 Rue Réaumur, Paris 75002
Ph: 01 42 33 52 92
Metro: Sentier
www.silk-thread.com
www.auverasoie.com

www.pecheasoie.com for silk fishing thread. Class dates and open evenings are listed on the website; look under "Agenda" or "Latest News", or visit the Au Ver a Soie Facebook Page.

NEIGHBOURHOOD NOTES

Rue Montorgueil

Don't miss taking a wander down Rue
Montorgueil. A lively street packed
with cafés and food vendors, the sights
and sounds add flavour to the culinary
delights you find here. Busy vendors
call out to friends in between singing
out the daily specials on their stands to
entice passers-by. The street has long
been associated with food; originally
home to the oyster markets where fresh
Brittany oysters were sold and popular
restaurants of the day like La Rocher
de Cancale, a favourite of Balzac and
his literary friends, served the slippery
delicacies. The restaurant of this name
at number 78 Rue Montorgueil opened
in 1846 taking the name from its popular
neighbour across the street that had
closed the year before. A pavement café
is the perfect spot for morning coffee,
lunch or afternoon apéro and to people-
watch Parisians and tourists alike. Visit
Stohrer, the oldest Paris patisserie, for a
Baba au Rhum or Paris Brest, their most
famous specialties. Rue Montorgueil is a
moveable feast at any time of the day.

SAJOU

The mandarine orange Sajou store stands out at number 47 Rue du Caire like a beacon among the sandstone buildings that densely populate the middle of Sentier. The colour feast continues inside the store where beautifully packaged sewing and embroidery notions, signature Sajou embroidery design cards, fabrics, patterned buttons, delicate thimbles and Fil au Chinois thread vie for detailed inspection.

Sajou is more than a beacon in a geographical sense; the story of its revival by Frédérique Crestin-Billet is remarkable. The original Maison Sajou established in 1828 had been a well-known and loved French brand but fell into decline. As an ardent collector of vintage haberdashery, Frédérique had already amassed a significant personal archive of Sajou picture catalogues and haberdashery pieces when she acquired the Sajou brand name in 2004 and launched her personal mission to revive the brand and restore the demand for quality French-made haberdashery. With expertise fuelled by passion she sought out artisan craftspeople with whom she could collaborate to re-establish notions production, artisan weavers to make classic cotton ribbons using traditional wooden looms and a woodworker from the Jura to fabricate fine boxes in the original Sajou style. She had the original Maison Sajou embroidery design cards reprinted using her personal archive as the design source then created new harmonious patterns to release.

Frédérique adored the Fil au Chinois brand of sewing thread with its beautiful picture designs and seized the opportunity to collaborate with its new owners to resume production of the historic thread. Frédérique recalls that it was perfect timing, she never imagined as a young collector that she would have the opportunity to work on such a project and that the product designs would come from her archives.

As Sajou celebrates its tenth anniversary under Frédérique's helm the rebranding and heritage of this French industrial success story is stronger than ever. Sajou is a key participant in the *Cousu Main* television series (equivalent to *The Great British Sewing Bee* series in the UK) and other projects to tell Sajou's story are in the pipeline. Already a collection of designs based on the history of the Toile du Jouy fabric and the Bayeux Tapestry has been released as embroidery kits or pattern templates.

Maison Sajou's designs, patterns, threads, and *mercerie* items are authentic reproductions beautifully crafted in France by skilled artisans. Seen all together it is a vision to behold: charming, old-world creations underpinned by entrepreneurial accomplishment.

47 Rue du Caire, Paris 75002
Ph: 01 42 33 42 66
www.sajou.fr
Open: Monday to Saturday 10am to 6.30pm
Metro: Sentier

NEIGHBOURHOOD NOTES

Passage du Caire

Almost opposite Sajou on Place du Caire three figure heads depicting the Egyptian goddess Hathor mark the entrance to Passage du Caire. Enter for a glimpse into the world of garment wholesalers, label and ticketing suppliers, mannequin makers and shop fitters. One of the first to be built, Passage du Caire was developed in 1798 at the time when Napoleon Bonaparte's successful exploits in Egypt triggered a craze for all things Egyptian, including this covered shopping precinct that mimicked a Middle-Eastern bazaar.

LA DROGUERIE

Back in 1975 the area around Paris's formerly bustling food market – Les Halles – was in the midst of upheaval due to the market moving outside city walls. Rue du Jour, on the left flank of the imposing Basilica St Eustache, once stuffed with butcher shops, was void of its cheerful workers and small businesses. A family of three sisters, their brother and sister-in-law, already immersed in their chosen careers took a risk on a business enterprise and opened up a small notions shop, La Droguerie, at number 9.

The gamble paid off; the family formulated just the right recipe for success with beautiful designs for hand-crafted clothing, embellishments and jewellery that has made La Droguerie an icon of France's hand-made movement. At the outset, the shop was a narrow corridor selling beads, buttons and yarn off fittings that included butchers' hooks from its former occupants. Today it has doubled in size: two corridors joined together with a capacious area at the rear of the shop where tall shelves are stacked high with cones of bright coloured knitting yarn, and branches exist in nine other French cities as well as outlets in Japan. The founding family members remain involved in the business, styling and designing new collections for regular release. Among the legions of devoted clients La Droguerie welcomes celebrity designers as well as the fourth generation of their original regulars.

The butchers' hooks are still in use, displaying hanks of yarn and pretty sample swatches. Giant meat scales sit camouflaged behind a swathe of yarn, beads are sold by the ladle *(la louche)* or spoonful *(la mesure)* as if you are at a delicatessen. As little as 20g of yarn can be bought and the staff wind yarn into plump balls and advise on a pretty trim, button choice or ribbon to finish a project.

Buttons are a specialty here, including some small production runs from the 1960s. When one of the factories that made the interesting Rhodoid buttons was closing, La Droguerie bought the remaining stock; limited numbers are still available, but once sold that's it.

La Droguerie's designs include hand-knitted and hand-sewn garments for all ages; delightful outfits for babies and toddlers, eye-catching jewellery and ready-to-make kits with all the materials in exactly the right quantity needed – perfect for those in a hurry, or as a prized Paris souvenir.

9-11 Rue du Jour, Paris 75001
Ph: 01 45 08 93 27
www.ladroguerie.com
Open: Monday 2pm to 6.45pm,
Tuesday to Saturday 10.30am to 6.45pm
Metro: Les Halles

L'ATELIER

L'Atelier's two stores on Rue des Plantes in the 14th arrondissement cover the full spectrum of creative interests. At number 27 the self-service trays glisten with beads, pearls, metal chains in varying weights, fasteners and items for jewellery making, plus buttons, ribbons, trims and general notions for everybody.

A few doors along at number 13bis the great line-up of Norwegian-brand Drops yarn attracts knitters and crocheters, while sewing, patchwork and quilting enthusiasts are drawn to the materials from international fabric houses including Makower and Dashwood from the UK, Liberty of London and France Duval Stalla. There are sewing patterns by Aime comme Marie and Frou-Frou, plus knitting needles, crochet hooks and knitting notions to complete your project needs.

---

27 and 13bis Rue des Plantes, Paris 75014
Ph: 01 45 40 02 25 (#27) and
01 57 05 79 25 (#13)
www.atelierdelacreation.com
Open: Tuesday to Saturday 10am to 7pm
Metro: Alésia

PARIS PASSEMENTERIE

This showroom on Rue Condorcet in the ninth arrondissement is where Dominique and Alaa El Sayed hold samples of the beautiful braids, trims, tassels and elaborate curtain ties that are handmade in their Franco-Egyptian family's workshop.

Dominique's knack for tasteful decoration can be seen in little touches here and there in the showroom; pretty tassels with intricate threads decorate perfume bottles and small vases, a curtain tie back with its opulent tassel artfully spills out of a plain glass vase, and in another a coil of richly coloured braid transforms the ordinary glass container into an eye catching ornament. She credits her eye for artistry to the weekly lessons in the "beaux-arts" that her mother insisted on during Dominique's school years.

The family's passementerie business began around the time the Suez Canal opened in 1869 Egypt. European nobility including the Empress Eugenie, wife of Napoleon III, and heads of state were among the invited guests to the opening. Passementerie was in hot demand; opulent decoration was the interior design trend and every hotel built for the occasion spared nothing in the way of decorative furnishings.

The family business, now in its fourth generation, upholds traditional handmade techniques in their workshop where skilled craftsmen each specialise in one part of the process from dyeing raw threads – silk, cotton and wool – to twisting cords, making the tassel and creating the decorative stitches used on some designs.

Paris Passementerie works with international interior designers and stylists to supply passementerie for elegant residences and historic homes around the world and collaborates with experts in interior design history to recreate authentic "period rooms" such as the 18th Century Precious Objects rooms in the Sully Wing of the Louvre Museum.

Visitors to the Paris Passementerie showroom can buy remnants of fabric, braid and trim, elaborate buttons, and curtain tiebacks; anything from remnants of ornate passementerie to orders from their new catalogues. Small elegant tassels for embellishing keys and key rings, bags and cushions become treasured mementos from Paris.

1 Rue Condorcet, Paris 75009
Ph: 01 45 26 22 55
Email: passementerie.paris@orange.fr
Open: Monday to Friday 11am to 5pm
or by appointment
Metro: Poissonnière.

DECLERCQ PASSEMENTIERS

The headquarters of Declercq Passementiers on Rue Etienne Marcel, once a banana-ripening warehouse, now has a thoroughly distinguished look suitable for a sixth-generation family business of trimming-makers. Here, on the first Thursday of each month, the Declercq team welcomes visitors to their HQ for demonstrations of the traditional weaving and handwork techniques used to create beautiful embellishments.

You can be treated to a presentation, in French, of the archives of historic passementerie samples from the time of Louis XIV, to the flowery, feminine style loved by Queen Marie Antoinette and the imposing extravagant designs popular during the time of Napoleon III – the heyday of passementerie.

The demonstrations are fascinating to watch: from weaving braids on the manually operated loom, to age-old skills at the handwork table for creating the individual elements of large elaborate pieces, to nimble fingers as they comb, twist and wrap threads, tie invisible knots and finally snip to reveal perfect furnishing baubles. Even the language intrigues: the seductively named *embrasse* is a curtain tieback and delicate *bouffettes* are pompoms.

The persistence of time-honoured techniques for making trimmings should not be mistaken for out-dated manufacture. At Declercq Passementiers tradition embraces innovation. Tassels, cords and braid using fibre-optic threads are the latest addition to their glamorous designs. With such comprehensive archives to draw on Declercq Passementiers is often commissioned to work on the restoration of historic interiors, supplying embellishments for the Château de Versailles, Fontainebleau, and Château Chantilly along with private residences, hotels and restaurants. Declercq Passementiers were awarded *Entreprise du Patrimoine Vivant* status by the French state, a mark to recognise the excellence of their ancestral passementerie know-how and production skills.

Declercq's head office showroom is open for visitors to view their extensive range of passementerie. Small items such as tassels and rosettes are available to purchase from stock while larger pieces such as tiebacks and braids can be ordered. If you are keen to make-it-yourself, Declercq's sell tassel kitsets in two different styles, each in a variety of colour-ways.

15 Rue Etienne Marcel, Paris 75001
Ph: 01 44 76 90 70
www.declercqpassementiers.fr
Open: 9am to 6pm Monday to Friday
Telephone in advance to reserve a place for the open day presentation.
Metro: Etienne Marcel

NEIGHBOURHOOD NOTES

Galerie Vivienne

Today every inch of Galerie Vivienne
is again a vision of neo-classical
elegance where modern-day *flâneurs*
can browse fashion stores including
Wolff et Descourtis's splendid patterned
silk, cashmere and wool shawls, John
Paul Gaultier's showroom, an antique
book store, cafes and restaurants. The
businessman who developed this beautiful
shopping arcade in 1826 called his
masterpiece a gallery rather than a passage;
passages were too popular, and this was a
special project. Galerie Vivienne opened
with tailors, a draper and haberdasher,
cobblers, a confectioner, a print seller and
a wine merchant doing business in elegant
neo-classical ambience. Goddesses and
nymphs adorned the walls of the rotunda,
light streamed in through the glass ceiling
dappling the resplendent mosaic-tiled
floor, it was a commercial success right
until the end of the 19th century. For an
absolute treat, stop for lunch or a late
afternoon glass of wine at Legrand Filles et
Fils gourmet food and wine merchants, or
select a few chocolates for later.

Entrances on Rue Vivienne, Rue de la
Banque or Rue des Petits Champs,
Paris 75002.

ADDRESSES TO STASH

For ribbons and trim

Shindo

The ribbon art window displays at Shindo's Paris showroom are almost as much of a landmark as the nearby Place des Victoires statue of Louis XIV. All Shindo ribbon products are available here, from beautiful ribbons in every colour imaginable, stripes and checks, festive patterns and braids to lingerie lace and hi-tech cords. The showroom staff speak fluent English and the minimum cut is one metre.

2 Rue d'Aboukir, Paris 75002
www.shindo.com
Open: Monday to Friday 10am to 6pm
Metro: Sentier

Mokuba

Japanese ribbon maker Mokuba offers a fabulous range of ribbons made of silk, satin, velvet, taffeta, organdie, leather, suede and linen, each of which can be pleated, ruffled, silver coated, elasticised, beaded, bobbled, sequinned, braided, double-sided and folded – and that is just for starters. Browse row upon row for jacquard ribbons, flower trims, braids and silk ribbons for embroidery while keeping an eye out to watch the graceful ballet-like movements when staff measure and cut ribbon. Ask to be taken across the courtyard for Broderie Anglaise and lace edgings. Note that two prices are shown for each ribbon reference number – TTC denotes the retail price.

18 Rue Montmartre, Paris 75001
Open: Monday to Friday 9.30am to 6.30pm
Metro: Les Halles

For beads

Matière Première

Beads, Swarovski, Bohemian glass, chains, jewellery patterns and charts, bead smith tools, tutorials. Grab a wicker basket and choose your beads to make a design yourself or have it made for you.

12 Rue de Sévigné, Paris 75004
www.matierepremiere.fr
Open: Monday to Saturday 11am to 7.30pm, Sunday 3pm to 7pm
Metro: Saint-Paul

Tout à Loisirs

(formerly La Compagnie des Perles)

This bead wholesaler's retail boutique conjures up the sense of being in a candy store where dozens of shapely glass jars sparkle with beads and counter displays bulge with colourful trinkets and baubles. Select your own from the huge range of beads, fantasy beads, semi-precious stones, findings and more.

50 Rue des Archives, Paris 75004
www.toutaloisirs.fr
Open: Monday to Friday 9am to 1pm, 2pm to 6pm
Metro: Hôtel de Ville or Saint-Paul or Rambuteau

For lace, ribbons and buttons

Entrée des Fournisseurs

Set in the heart of the historic Marais district this boutique tucked away in a quiet courtyard offers an excellent selection of beautiful lace and buttons, including a collection of white, cream and pearl shades for wedding dress embellishment. There is a small range of knitting yarns from Fonty and Plassard, fabrics from Atelier Brunette and Liberty along with linens, cottons, tulle, frog fastenings and general sewing notions. Although many Marais-district shops are open on Sundays, Entrée des Fournisseurs is not.

8 Rue des Francs Bourgeois, Paris 75003
Ph 01 48 87 58 98
www.lamercerieparisienne.com
Open: Monday to Saturday 10.30am to 7pm
Metro: Saint-Paul or Chemin Vert

"This beautiful city is a marvellous place to hunt out lace, textiles, home embroidered fabrics and countless treasures from bygone days."

VINTAGE &
SHABBY CHIC

Fashion is woven into the history of Paris more than any other city. This beautiful city is a marvellous place to hunt out old lace, textiles, hand-embroidered fabrics and countless treasures from bygone days. While looking for treasures is fun in itself, there is nothing quite as satisfying as restoring and reusing old fabrics to reveal their former beauty and return value to once-precious materials.

The pieces that can be found in the antique and *brocante* boutiques, flea markets and regular neighbourhood *vide-grenier* markets are perfect for anyone with a dash of imagination and a few handcraft skills to customise clothing, repurpose for a practical household use or create a special interior decor piece.

ATELIER LA CLARIÈRE

Inside this beautiful little workshop it's as if time has stopped and been captured in a gentle dream. Soft coloured vintage linens and lace, mother-of-pearl buttons, dusky pink ribbons all salvaged from Parisian flea markets have been expertly revived and up-cycled into chic decorative items and romantic-styled clothing for children and adults.

At La Clarière antique fabric and lace materials are for sale along with a selection of vintage decorative items; vases, kitchen ware, ornaments and handmade creations including lavender pouches, cushions, market bags, table linens, nightwear and clothing.

The atelier is owned and run by Sharon Macdonald. She has an eye for detail that stems from her architecture training in her native Canada and many years' experience working in the field of interiors. Her atelier reflects her skill in creating the perfect old-world-chic look. Sharon makes the items for sale in the boutique herself, and creates custom pieces on commission. She knows what to look for when searching *vide-grenier*

stalls and how to prepare old linen and lace fabrics that "set her heart racing". Her passion is to give new and useful life to once-cherished lace and woven materials that would otherwise be left forgotten in the back of dusty old cupboards. With an impeccable sense of style and perfectionist workmanship, she creates unique pieces that are as beautiful as once before.

8 Rue de l'Esperance, Paris 75013
Ph: 01 82 09 44 79
www.laclariere.blogspot.fr online sales through **www.etsy.com/shop/laclariere**
Open: Wednesday to Saturday noon to 7pm.
Metro: Corvisart or Place d'Italie

CHEZ DENTELLE

Being passionate about old lace and clothing, Shigeko, the owner of Chez Dentelle, could not believe her good fortune when she first arrived in Paris from Japan almost thirty years ago and discovered the quality of the lace she saw. She began collecting pieces from all over Europe and found she couldn't stop, so turned her collection into a boutique, selling the pieces that she has hunted down.

Taking up a mere eight square metres of space on Rue Rambuteau, Chez Dentelle must be one of the tiniest shops in Paris. It is like a secret wardrobe: open the door carefully, step through and find yourself amid a remarkable collection of exquisite antique lace treasures. Among shirts with lace ruffles, lace bed linen, trims, lace collars and stoles are delicate silk and lace nightgowns for sylph-like figures from another decade. Shigeko's most cherished discoveries are the fine 18th-century Belgian needle lace pieces.

All pieces at Chez Dentelle are for sale, from complete antique garments to dainty lace gloves and handkerchiefs, while lace trims and antique fabric are sold by the metre. Shigeko is a wise collector and willingly shares her advice on looking after antique lace materials.

16 Rue Rambuteau, Paris 75003
Ph: 01 42 74 02 51
Open: Tuesday to Saturday 11am to 5.30pm, sometimes closed at lunchtime.
Metro: Rambuteau
No credit cards

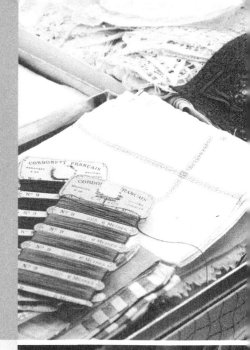

NEIGHBOURHOOD NOTES

The Place Pompidou in front of the Pompidou Centre, home of the French National Museum of Modern Art, is a lively place to see street performers in action. On the river (south) side of the museum is the Stravinsky Fountain on Place Igor Stravinsky. Admire the sculptures by well-known artists Niki de Saint Phalle and Jean Tinguely. The former's colourful figures have inspired many amigurumi crocheters.

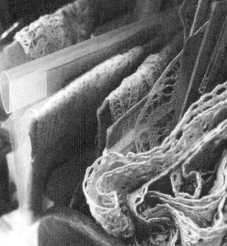

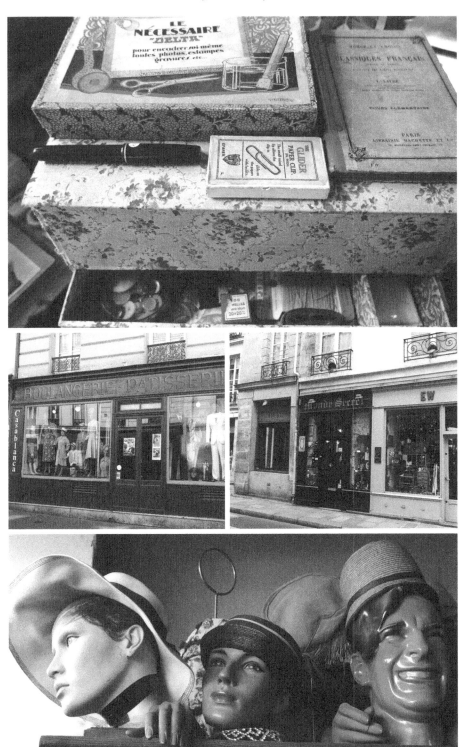

ADDRESSES TO STASH

Casablanca

Swing by Casablanca in the 11th arrondissement for quality vintage fabrics from the 1930s and 40s through to the 70s. Casablanca's owner, Najat, sources fabric from the past to make vintage-style clothing for theatre and film; men's suits in snazzy pin stripes with half belts and back vents, cream suits and matching newsboy caps. Casablanca's supply of vintage fabric is perfect for making tea dresses and suits.

17 Rue Moret, Paris 75011
Ph: 06 64 27 90 15
Open: Monday to Saturday 2pm to 7pm
Online sales through **www.etsy.com/ shop/casablancashopparis**
Metro: Ménilmontant or Rue Saint-Maur

Au Petit Bonheur La Chance

For an enjoyable time browsing, visit Rue Saint Paul in the fourth arrondissement. This quaint little street is part of Village Saint Paul, an area known for its *brocante* and antique boutiques.

Au Petit Bonheur la Chance is brimful with colourful vintage crockery, fabric, tea towels, handkerchiefs, patterns, lace, braid, buttons, children's toys and games, postcards and much more. The owner is a relentless and talented *chineur* – an antique hunter – who sources stock from flea markets and *vide-greniers*.

Au Petit Bonheur la Chance
13 Rue Saint Paul, Paris 75004
Ph: 01 42 74 36 38 or 06 62 61 79 95
Open: Tuesday to Saturday 11am to 1pm and 2.30pm to 7pm
Metro: Saint-Paul

EW

Along Rue Saint Paul at EW the artfully displayed mix of delightful pieces holds you spellbound. Scraps of vintage fabric, needle cases, sewing kits and antique samplers nestled amongst pretty lamps, old crockery and small pieces of household furniture exude a warm and welcoming ambience for unhurried browsing.

EW, 21 Rue Saint-Paul, Paris 75004
Ph: 01 42 77 55 11
Open: Thursday to Monday 11am to 1pm, 2.30pm to 7pm, closed Tuesday and Wednesday.
Metro: Saint-Paul

Flea markets and neighbourhood *vide-grenier* markets provide fun opportunities to hunt for cast-off treasures.

Vide grenier markets

Vide grenier literally means attic-emptying; it's the equivalent of car-boot sales, trunk sales, or garage sales. Search online for listings of specialty markets *mercerie, broderie* or markets described as *Puces des Couturières*. These are one-off markets of second-hand fabrics, patterns, notions, and yarn where former haberdashers sell off their stock, vintage collectors lighten their load and crafters destash.

A site that lists upcoming textile flea markets in all regions is:
www.coutureonline.fr/agenda-de-la-couture/agenda-puces-des-couturieres.html

Permanent flea markets in Paris

Marché aux Puces at Vanves
www.pucesdevanves.com

This market is held every Saturday and Sunday morning from 7am to about 2pm; be aware they may pack up early. Stalls line Avenue Marc Sangnier and Avenue Georges Lafenestre offering a tantalising array of anything and everything. Some merchants set up stalls every week in the same spot like Julia who sells vintage *mercerie* under her *Missy* label, others appear once or twice a month, many have done business here for years and years. Small treasures, textiles, lace and paper pieces, buttons and jewellery that can be carried home easily await the gaze of those who stroll along the avenue gently picking their way through the past.

Metro: Porte de Vanves, follow the signs for Marché aux Puces.

Marché aux Puces at St Ouen

This market is held every Saturday, Sunday and Monday. Stalls open between 9 and 10am and continue to 6pm. It's huge: 1700 merchants in 14 separate markets, plus delightful cafes, live music – gypsy jazz – and treasures galore. With all the atmosphere of a fairground; masses of everything from bric-a-brac to high-end antiques are on offer with merchants as interesting as the goods they sell. Stalls of vintage notions and fabric cluster on *Allées* (Aisles) 1, 4 and 7 near the Rue Rosier entrance of the Vernaison sector. Other stalls selling textile, lace, passementerie and haberdashery items may be found in the Malassis markets and in Le Passage between Rue Lécuyer and Rue Jules Vallès.

www.marcheauxpuces-saintouen.com
Metro: Porte de Clignancourt or Garibaldi, follow the signs.

Emmaüs charity boutiques

This international charity organisation, founded in 1949 by France's beloved Abbé Pierre, provides shelter and work for the homeless. In France there is a network of *friperies*; boutiques that sell cheap second-hand clothes and goods. These three suburban stores specialise in vintage and second-hand haberdashery materials. Special sales and events are announced on the Emmaüs Boutiques' Facebook page.

The suburban haberdasheries are open the first and third Saturday of each month only:

La Petite Mercerie, 45 Avenue Lefèvre, Le Plessis-Trévise 94420.

Emmaüs Mercerie et Retro, 15 Boulevard Louis Armand, Neuilly sur Marne 93330.

Emmaüs de Port Marly Bougival, 7 Ile de la Loge, Le Port Marly 78380

Auctions

In the 16 amazing sale rooms at the Drouot auction house, you can sometimes find lace and textiles, needlework collectibles; thimbles, needle cases and the like among the auction lots. For a pleasant diversion, visit during viewing time when amateur collectors and professionals alike busily scribble notes in their catalogues before sale time.

www.drouot.com for sales, catalogues, viewing and auction times
9 Rue Drouot, Paris 75009
Open: Monday to Friday 11am to 6pm and certain Saturdays and Sundays.
Metro: Richelieu-Drouot

FLEA MARKET PHOTOGRAPHY ETIQUETTE

In our experience, it's okay to... before taking a photo of a vendor's stall. Start with a polite greeting, *Bonjour Madame* or *Monsieur*... some in English a the vendor, at these markets encounter thousands of tourists, so why not make the extra effort and try in French. *Je voudrais prendre des photos, s'il vous plaît.* I'd like to take some photos please... The vendors will most often allow it, occasionally not, and be appreciative that you asked. Certainly you'll find them more positively disposed towards you when there's any bargaining over the price of a souvenir that has caught your eye... the same politeness applies in both cases and we suggest a greet first and ask permission to take photos.

GLOSSARY AND TRANSLATION

Antique – Strictly speaking refers to items older than 100 years from present day.

Brocante – French word for bric-a-brac, junk stores.

Cartonnage – Decorative box making.

Chineur – Person browsing flea markets for treasures.

Ciseaux lingère, ciseaux à broder, ciseaux tailleur – Household or sewing scissors, embroidery scissors, tailors' shears.

Couturière – Seamstress, dressmaker, sewist.

Depôt-vente – A consignment store where second-hand clothes are sold on-behalf of the owner. Some depôt-vente stores specialise in designer labels.

Drapery – An old-fashioned word for a fabric store.

Droguerie – A shop where bits and bobs of household goods are sold.

Echeveau – A skein or hank of yarn.

Encyclopaedia of Needlework – Book first published 1886 by Thérèse de Dillmont. Old copies can be found in flea markets. New editions can still be found through booksellers.

Faire soi-même, Faire moi-même – To make it oneself, to make it myself, to do it oneself.

Fait main – Handmade.

Fil au Chinois thread – French made sewing thread famous for packaging with Chinese-themed pictures.

Findings – Small supplies and tools for jewellery, bag making etc.

Flâneur – Person who strolls at leisure.

Friperie – Shops selling cheap second-hand clothing.

Frivolité – Tatting.

Gross uniquement – Wholesale only.

Haberdashery, Haberdasher – Shop selling needles, thread buttons, trim, ribbons, etc. Also called a *mercerie* (Fr), or a notions store (US). A merchant whose business is a haberdashery.

Haute couture – Luxury fashion, unique one-off items.

Mercerie – French name for a store where buttons, tools, trims and threads for needlecrafts are sold. Same as Haberdashery (Eng), Notions store (US).

Métier – Occupation, job, profession, trade. Also the word for a weaving loom.

Notions store – North American term for a store where buttons, tools, trims and threads for needlecrafts are sold. Same as Haberdashery (Eng), *mercerie* (Fr).

Particulier – Individual person as opposed to a professional.

Pas de détail – No retail sales.

Passementerie – Decorative trims for furnishings and uniforms such as tassels, braids, fringes and pompoms.

Pelote – A ball of yarn for knitting or crochet.

Quincallerie – Similar to a droguerie.

Savoir faire – Know how.

Technical fabric – A generic term for manmade fabrics with special qualities initially used in industries then adopted by clothing designers.

Tricot, tricoteuses, tricot soirée – Knitting, knitters, knit night.

Vide-grenier – Attic-emptying, equivalent to garage sales, car boot sale, street market.

Vide appartement or vide maison – Sale onsite at a private home or apartment.

Vintage – Genuine old article, previously limited to period from 1980s to present time, now loosely used to describe anything old and authentic. Beware of imitations.

Yarn – Any fibre spun and prepared for knitting, crochet, weaving. Includes wool, cashmere, mohair, alpaca, silk, cotton, linen, possum and yak.

STITCHING UP PARIS BY LOCATION

Key for goods available:
H = Haberdashery, E = Embroidery,
S = Sewing, K = Knitting, V = Vintage,

1st Arrondissement 75001

Declerq Passementiers Trims

La Droguerie H S K Beads

Mokuba Trims

Tapisserie de France E

2nd Arrondissement 75002

Au Ver à Soie E

Cat'Laine K

Courty et Fils Scissors

Episode Vintage V

Esmod S

Fil 2000 H

Hamon Scissors Tools

Lil Weasel K H S

Mon Atelier en Ville

Sajou H

Sentier fabric shops: Tissu Market, Sonitis, GHT Tissus, General Diff, Les Etoffes du Sentier S

Shindo Trims

Ultramod H

3rd Arrondissement 75003

Chez Dentelles V

Entrée des Fournisseurs H K

IE S

Musée des Arts et Métiers

Musée Carnavalet

Weber Métaux K

4th Arrondissement 75004

Au Petit Bonheur La Chance V

Centre Pompidou

EW V

Matière Première Beads

Petit Pan S

Phildar K

Tout à Loisirs Beads

5th Arrondissement 75005

Cluny Musée National du Moyen Age

Phildar K

Une Maille à L'Endroit K

6th Arrondissement 75006

France Duval Stella S

9th Arrondissement 75009

Le Bonheur des Dames, Passage Verdeau boutique E

Le Comptoir K H S

Drouot Auction House V

Paris Passementerie Trims

Phildar K

10th Arrondissement 75010

Les Tricoteurs Volants K

11th Arrondissement 75011

Baeyens Findings

Brin de Cousette S

Les Brodeuses Parisiennes E

Casablanca V

Cousine K

La Croix et la Manière E

Inès Patchwork S

12th Arrondissement 75012
Le Bonheur des Dames E
Malhia Kent S K

13th Arrondissement 75013
La Clarière V
La Bien Aimée K
L'OisiveThé K
Galerie des Gobelins

14th Arrondissement 75014
L'Atelier de la Création H S K
Vanves Flea Market V

15th Arrondissement 75015
L'Aiguille-en-Fête stitching fair K S E
Créations et Savoir-faire craft fair K S E
Une Maille à L'Endroit K

16th Arrondissement 75016
Musée Marmottan Monet
Sevilla S

17th Arrondissement 75017
Une Maille à L'Endroit K

18th Arrondissement 75018
Bergère de France K
Dam Boutons Buttons
Frou-Frou Mercerie Contemporaine S H
K H Afrique Mode S
Montmartre fabric shops: Dreyfus Marché St Pierre, Tissus Reine, Sacrés Coupons, Karin Sajo, Tissu Market S
Les Petits Points Parisiens K S
Tricot Saint Pierre K

Suburbs
Emmaüs Mercerie V
Musée de la Toile de Jouy
St Denis Musée d'Art et d'Histoire
St Ouen Flea Market V

INDEX OF SHOPS A - Z

Acknowledgements

This book could not have been written without the guiding hand of our wonderful editor, Lizzie Harwood of www.editordeluxe.com. She shepherded us through version after version right to the end, untangling the knots in our stories and checking the finishing touches with patience and good humour. We are very grateful.

We owe enormous thanks to our designers Carina Brasell and Aleisha Findlay at www.littlerocket.co.nz who gathered up our words, photographs and ideas and stitched them together beautifully.

We thank the many shop owners who cheerfully gave up their time to answer our questions and allowed us to photograph every corner of their stores. It was a great pleasure to meet with each of them and hear their stories. We extend a big thank you to the shop assistants, warehouse staff and market stall vendors for the friendly welcome they extend to Stitching up Paris tours and their willingness to share their savoir-faire (know-how) in English. The ongoing conversations we have about stitching are a delight.

Lightning Source UK Ltd
Milton Keynes UK
UKOW07f0338250216

269087UK00010B/33/P

9 782955 506608